Interviewing
in Depth

To
My Wife Sharon
Daughter Alexis Georgia
and in Memory of My Mother

Interviewing in Depth

The
Interactive-Relational
Approach

John T. Chirban

SAGE Publications
International Educational and Professional Publisher
Thousand Oaks   London   New Delhi

For information address:

 SAGE Publications, Inc.
2455 Teller Road
Thousand Oaks, California 91320
E-mail: order@sagepub.com

SAGE Publications Ltd.
6 Bonhill Street
London EC2A 4PU
United Kingdom

SAGE Publications India Pvt. Ltd.
M-32 Market
Greater Kailash I
New Delhi 110 048 India

Printed in the United States of America

Library of Congress Cataloging-in-Publication Data

Chirban, John T.
    Interviewing in depth: The interactive-relational approach/
author, John T. Chirban.
    Includes bibliographical references and index.
    ISBN 0-8039-7317-9 (cloth: acid-free paper).—ISBN
0-8039-7318-7 (pbk.: acid-free paper)
    1. Interviewing. I.Title.
BF637.I5C49 1996
158'.39—dc20   96-4475

This book is printed on acid-free paper.

96 97 98 99 10 9 8 7 6 5 4 3 2 1

Sage Production Editor: Gillian Dickens
Cover Design: Candice Harman

Contents

Acknowledgments

Preparing this book has been a very reflective and intimate experience because understanding what constitutes a significant relationship is critical for effective interviewing. I wish to acknowledge those who have influenced my life—those responsible for shaping who I am, thereby fostering my search to unravel the mystery of what constitutes a significant relationship.

I dedicate this book to my wife Sharon, my daughter Alexis Georgia, and to the memory of my mother in recognition of their help in offering me essential interactions and relationships. My experiences with them generated powerful dimensions to my understanding of life and effective communication.

I especially thank my parents, from whom I learned sincerity, morality, and love.

I acknowledge my mentors who influenced this book: at Harvard University, Dr. B. F. Skinner; at Boston University, Dr. Anthony G. Barrand, Rosanna Warren, and Dr. G. Rita Dudley Grant, who encouraged me through their sensitive souls and penetrating minds to articulate my approach in interviewing.

My list of acknowledgments also includes relationships that have emerged from my interviews. As evidenced in this book, Lucille Ball and B. F. Skinner, especially, have had a powerful effect on my work and life. Additionally, I thank Desi Arnaz, Jr., for his willingness to review the manuscript of my interviews with his mother, Lucille Ball, during the painful period following her death.

With special reference to the preparation of this manuscript for publication, I am deeply indebted to Ed Keane and my wife, Sharon. Ed has served as a manager for several of my writing projects and has offered invaluable counsel in the refinements of this manuscript. Sharon not only prompted me to publish this manuscript but provided thoughtful and insightful commentary to shape this book. Without their direct involvement, love, and support, this would not have been possible.

From Sage Publications, I particularly acknowledge the trust and care afforded me by my editor, Mr. Jim Nageotte. Jim's professionalism, sound judgment, and expertise enabled this work to reach its audience. Additionally, I thank the Sage staff for their assistance in facilitating the many details required to publish this book.

Finally, I express appreciation to colleagues who commented on specific parts of this book, and my students, who have implemented ideas set forth here and responsibly shared with me their findings. Much gratitude is due for the patience and perseverance of Janice Romano in preparing this manuscript.

Foreword

This is a book about deeper listening. It is a book that will help professionals become more sensitive and enable closer communication in the interview. John Chirban is clearly a teacher and a leader—I hope that many of us will join him in his journey of understanding and caring.

Chirban's interactive-relational approach does two major things for us in terms of interview practice. First, it is a clearly stated model that can help us all to think about the interview in new and more complete ways. Second, it seems to me the best work that I have seen illustrating how to reach that second or "inner level" with our clients. It is here we touch the innermost self and have the opportunity to view others with authenticity.

I am thankful that Dr. Chirban has brought us face to face with B. F. Skinner, the person. Skinner was a model for my own professional growth. I had the good fortune to have several contacts with him, although not in the same depth as Dr. Chirban. Skinner was a complete and fine human being. He was not the stereotype of the cold scientist but, rather, was a caring and highly involved person. Chirban's interviews with Skinner are important historically for our field.

Lucille Ball is another icon, albeit in a very different field from Skinner. I found myself reading and rereading John Chirban's interview with her. Lucille Ball's life experience comes dramatically alive in her time with Dr. Chirban. I recommend reading this book more than once. There is something about the interviews that engage the reader and suggest the need for more.

This book is a must for professionals. It is also a book that could complement many courses in counseling and psychotherapy, and it will be helpful to beginners. Dr. Chirban shows us both how and why we interview. *Interviewing in Depth: The Interactive-Relational Approach* will hold an important place on my shelf. I hope you find it as warm and fascinating as I have.

Allen E. Ivey, Ed.D., A.B.P.P.
Distinguished University Professor
University of Massachusetts, Amherst

Introduction

An interview, in the true sense of the word, gives an "inner view" of the interviewed person. *The Oxford English Dictionary* traces the etymology of the word *interview* to Middle French and to Latin "from *entre-voir,* to have a glimpse of, *s'entrevoir,* to see each other, from *entré + voir:* Latin *videre* to see." I use this term to signify the active search for a full understanding of a person's life—"the inner view." Comprehending the essence of an individual, his or her emotions, motivations, and needs, is the central task. Through introducing an approach for open and earnest communication where both participants express their thoughts and feelings, *Interviewing in Depth: The Interactive-Relational Approach* enables the interviewer to achieve an effective in-depth interview. In the end, this book prepares the reader to put the interactive-relational (I:R) approach into action.

Interviewing has become increasingly valued in modern life; it is an essential tool in psychology, journalism, the health professions, and business. As such, interviews have the potential to convey the power of life inherent in human contact. However, many interviewing approaches reduce the process to fact-finding ventures. Approaches to interviewing that ignore or overlook the dynamics between interviewer and interviewee often result in lifeless or less than effective interviewing.

The scientific method, the method of choice of our technological age, has found its way into and even dominates contemporary interviewing approaches. Scientific approaches, which focus primarily on the collection of empirical data, often lack vitality and fail to communicate what one can do to capture the essence of a person and to reveal insights by and about relationships. Such analytical forms of interviewing disregard the human dimension of an encounter, neglecting the heart-to-heart, as well as face-to-face, elements.

Formal, traditional approaches to interviewing often place distance between interviewers and their interviewees, predisposing the interviewer to assess the interviewee: to generalize, to embellish, to exaggerate, to stereotype, and to simplify. As a result, these approaches do not provide a complete and accurate picture of the participants' contributions, motives, involvement, strengths, and weaknesses. The dynamics of the interaction and relationship, when tapped, provide the most revealing portrait of an interviewee.

The struggle to conduct an empirically focused interview versus a relational interview often creates a dilemma for the interviewer. On one hand, clinical or professional posturing may subordinate the interviewee to gather data. On the other hand, a personable and engaging posture may render an interview that lacks objective facts. Because some may view an interview approach that includes a developed relational dimension as unproductive or unprofessional, the interviewer may opt for a more formal, impersonal approach to resolving this dilemma.

One need not sacrifice a professional interview, however, when one is relational. Holstein and Gubrium (1995) observe, "Highly refined interview technologies streamline, standardize, and sanitize the process, but, despite their methodological sophistication, they persistently ignore the most fundamental of epistemological questions: Where does this knowledge come from, and how is it derived?" (p. 2). By developing an interactive and relational stance, an interviewer may establish an appropriate professional posture and, significantly, understand more of the interviewee than possible with an empirical approach. In fact, by drawing upon personal resourcefulness, the interviewer may access information that would not emerge through formal questioning alone. The components of one's resourcefulness reside in the use of personal characteristics and the qualities applied to the interaction and relationship.

The interaction creates a context or setting for the wellspring of engaging an interviewee. Usually initiated by the interviewer, the interaction shapes the dynamics, the conscious and unconscious processes, of communication that evolves between the interviewer and interviewee. The interaction often determines the role and parameters for communication, accounting for the balance of power and freedom experienced in the interview process.

The relationship provides the vehicle for the interviewer to know the interviewee. This relationship emerges from the deepening awareness of one another that occurs in their interactions, that in turn becomes the source of the energy in the interview. Within this relationship, the two people exchange their ideas, beliefs, and feelings that enhance growth and understanding.

This perspective radically contrasts with approaches toward interviewing that discourage the relationship and fundamentally implement techniques. The I:R approach, through the interaction and relationship, provides a plan for attaining a goal as well as a way to maintain a constructive relational dynamic. In this way, an interviewer does not forfeit the accumulation of data but gains greater clarity, insight, and depth.

This approach identifies the qualities that explicate the *interaction* and *relationship* between the interviewer and interviewee, rendering the inner view. The I:R approach necessitates the inclusion and consideration of both parties. It invites the interviewer and interviewee to share their experiences genuinely and to relate to one another. It also requires the interviewer to address his or her objectives and to incorporate those personal resources that encourage and support reciprocal involvement.

Origins of the I:R Approach

The I:R approach resulted from my years of longitudinal interviews with 12 leading American women who had agreed to participate in a project titled "Women, Motivation and Success" (Chirban, 1990). When I began, I intended to conduct conventional interviews. I designed a questionnaire to standardize my work according to traditional qualitative research methods. Because of the *interaction* that evolved between each woman and me, the formally structured questionnaire proved awkward in our meetings and created an obstacle to our work. Therefore, I decided simply to speak less formally, weaving previously formulated questions directly into the course of our *relationship.* As a result, the particular qualities in the interaction and relationship that emerged fueled our encounters.

In fact, in the process of our discussions, not only did we address the originally formulated questions, but I also obtained a penetrating, comprehensive understanding of these women. The women spoke candidly; more than that, they wondered, reflected, and, by their admission, discovered more about themselves. Had I asked only the formulated questions, the women would have probably remained in expected celebrity stereotypes. However, our interactions and relationships illuminated startling facts and poignant emotions that broke predictable images. Through this approach, they shared fascinating experiences and exhibited an investment in their interviews.

To portray the women, I struggled with a variety of traditional biographical and thematic formats that did not reflect what was ascertained through the interaction and relationship. Academic and popular approaches failed to capture and reveal the women. In one effort to account for the revelations and shared experiences, I presented profiles of their lives. This format described information drawn from our meetings and similar to biographical essays. However, this method omitted the process that generated the women's rich and spontaneous insights. Another method was to discuss specific themes such as the role of father, mother, or love, that ran through the lives of all these women. This approach, too, was deficient in capturing what the women had shared. Something was always missing.

Lucille Ball was one of the participants in the original study. A discussion with Lucy's son, Desi Arnaz, Jr., confirmed my feelings. After reading some of the material, Desi remarked, "Something's missing! Your heart and love that I experience when I talk with you is reduced and blocked." Desi prompted me to reconsider the presentation of the interviews with Lucy.

Reviewing the taped conversations, I found the true strength of the interviews rested in the shared interaction and relationship of the interview process. It propelled the experience and unlocked a deeper understanding of the subject. Through analyzing the interview process, the dynamics of the interaction and the relational experience emerged; the I:R approach became apparent. Unique access and insights arose both for and about these women. I realized that I, as every other interviewer, establish a particular experience through the interaction and the quality of the relationship. These elements that capture an interview are fundamental to the I:R approach.

I later recognized that the same characteristics of this approach pervaded the weekly taped conversations that I had with B. F. Skinner concerning behaviorism and its relationship to philosophy and religion. To popular thought, few subjects would seem as unrelated as B. F. Skinner and religion. However, the very elements of the I:R dynamics allowed me to engage him in detailed discussions of faith, God, and spirituality and to observe him working through the meanings of these issues in his life and work.

Noteworthy to the effectiveness of this approach, Skinner acknowledged that he had neither participated in such dialogue nor ever maintained such continuous academic communication with anyone else. At one point, commenting about our weekly work that extended over a 5-year period, he wrote, "I believe that together we are developing a theme of considerable importance in a way that has had no earlier treatment" (B. F. Skinner, personal correspondence, June 30, 1989).

In addition to selected interviews with Lucille Ball and B. F. Skinner,[1] this book includes segments of case studies from interviews and discussions from my private practice and research. The case study approach shows how the I:R interviewing technique results in learning about the interviewee's world by revealing specific elements of the interaction and relationship as they occurred.

The I:R approach requires the interviewer's (a) self-awareness, (b) authenticity, (c) attunement, (d) posturing in the interaction, (e) engagement of relational dynamics, and (f) integration of his or her person in the process of interviewing. Through these components, the interviewer tailors the I:R approach accordingly to achieve the goals of an interview.

This I:R approach explains how self-awareness engenders greater self-confidence for the interviewer; it shows how authenticity promotes a genuine exchange of thoughts and feelings; it details how attunement enables the interviewer to enter into the world of the interviewee; it explains how posturing affects roles and exchanges in an interaction; it reveals how engagement of the relational dynamic encourages an open and genuine discussion; and it explains how the interviewer's characteristics, beliefs, and values have a significant and unique impact on the interviewee.

The I:R approach emphasizes the critical importance of both the *interaction* and the *relationship*. It identifies the particular qualities that deepen an interview. The interviewer comes in direct contact with and participates in the interviewee's personality, struggles, search, and vision—elements that the interviewer might neither feel nor recognize using traditional interview techniques.

This book shows how the I:R approach may apply in various fields. Although based on psychological perspectives and drawing on psychological constructs, this technique for interviewing is applicable in many interviewing settings. It will also help interviewers to assess how their personal characteristics affect their work, become aware of their posturing and relational styles, and effectively integrate themselves into the process of interviewing.

This book provides a context for the role of the interaction and relationship in view of different interviewing theories with reference to the psychoanalytic, behavioral, and humanistic schools. It describes the roles and characteristics that the interviewer brings to an interview, and it prepares the reader to apply the I:R approach.

Each interviewer has the responsibility of seeking clarity about the subjective and objective impact on his or her work. To a great extent, the interviewer's approach in an interview serves as a transparency of his or her personal qualities. This approach assumes the interviewer's preparation (competency concerning the subject of the interview) and his or her implementation of effective communication skills learned from basic interviewing studies. This approach presumes that the interviewer has the interest to grow in self-awareness and to make the most of the interview experience. Authentic communication and attunement follows through one's self-awareness and integration of personal qualities. In this way, reciprocity can occur with the interviewee and provide for a continually deepening knowledge of him or her.

Each interviewer needs to identify and incorporate his or her personal characteristics into the process to allow his or her full participation in the interview. Likewise, the interviewer's approach may be reflected in terms of personal values and commitments. Rather than perceiving personal feelings as an obstacle (i.e., one causing harm in the interaction), the I:R approach suggests recognition and management of such feelings. Through this approach, one may learn to integrate the self into the interviewing process.

In the final analysis, one's person, more than one's theory or technique, allows one to see another person. We may judge the quality of an interview according to the degree that we relate to one another and what we share through the interaction and relationship.

Note

1. Written consent to present the taped verbatims of Lucille Ball and B. F. Skinner have been obtained from Ms. Ball and Dr. Skinner.

1

Identifying the
Interactive-Relational Approach

Case Study—The Person of a Prisoner

As a psychologist for the Massachusetts prison system, I learned in a triage meeting that the administration planned to move a prisoner named Randy to a maximum security facility because they feared he would become violent in reaction to his father's sudden death. Because *my* father had just died, I could not help but associate with Randy's loss. I wondered whether he felt devastated by his father's death.

Although the senior clinicians recognized that Randy was grieving, they smiled at my suggestion to reconsider this move, believing that the planned safety measure was necessary to guard against his potentially aggressive response. Nevertheless, they agreed that I should interview the young man, cautioning me about his history of assault and battery. Because of his loss, I felt more concerned about his grief than his reputed dangerous nature. My readiness to attend to his emotional needs led me to approach him from a caring stance.

Randy was a rather imposing 23-year-old man: tall, well-built, and visibly distressed. Through a window, I saw him intensely pacing the floor. After greeting him, I asked him how he was managing. He responded, "They probably won't let me out of prison to go to the funeral." He added that if he were allowed to attend the funeral, guards would have to escort him in shackles and chains. Randy bemoaned the agony that this would bring his mother, quite possibly projecting his own disgrace. As we spoke about his concerns and the imminent move, I became convinced that relocating Randy would prove detrimental. As a result, I requested to meet with the superintendent. At this meeting, I suggested that he amend the order for shackles and chains as requisite for Randy's attendance at the funeral and that they not move Randy to the tighter facility.

In this interview, two points were evident to me: First, Randy needed concrete intervention in response to his crisis; and second, supportive action could set the stage to establish the basis for therapy. The superintendent saw my proposal as risky. However, after checking Randy's record in prison, which was excellent, he approved the recommendation with the stipulation that a two-man security escort accompany Randy to the funeral.

I did not learn of the outcome until I saw Randy again the following week. When we met for our scheduled session, he was subdued. I listened quietly as he recounted the painful steps of the funeral. He found it difficult to discuss his feelings. We agreed to meet the next day.

When we met, Randy was wired, not unlike at our first session. He informed me that after he had seen me last, the superintendent had called him to his office and told him that he should cry to express his grief. Randy stated that he felt like he was ordered to cry on the spot.

"I was not going to cry because he told me to," Randy said. "Why should I do this in front of him? He doesn't give a shit about me!" We talked for almost the full session about this incident. Toward the end of our hour, I shared my observation that we were discussing events but not his emotions directly. So, I asked him how he was feeling. He responded, "I actually figured that you would like to know what was going on inside me, so I want you to read these poems that I wrote." Handing me two poems, he quickly exited with a crack in his voice, saying, "I'll see you next week."

In his poems, Randy expressed powerful insight, warmth, and love for his dad. The poems were drafted as letters to his father in heaven. I was struck by his ability to reveal his vulnerability and to express passion and sensitivity.

When I met with Randy 1 week later, he appeared calm. In a boyish way, he asked, "So Doc, what do you think of my poems?" I told him that I was "very impressed." He said, "You know, I'm impressed with you, too." Randy continued, "Every time I see you, you sit on this side of the room."

Confused by Randy's observation, I asked him to explain. He pointed to the panic button behind the office therapist's chair and said, "I know that you're supposed to sit over there in case you need to call for emergency help, but *you* never do." I was surprised by his remark and asked him how he knew about the button. He quickly responded, "You know, I am an electrician by trade, and I installed the alarms!" We both laughed.

In following sessions, we spoke more directly about his anger, from his father's death to Randy's reaction to the superintendent's awkward attempt to show support. Randy gained insight into the basis for his aggressive behavior. Our conversations delved deeper into many other emotional experiences of his life that led him toward change. He developed successful friendships and intimacies as he began to express his feelings openly and directly. Over the course of our work he became goal directed in his preparation for a career where he could use his trade skills after serving his prison sentence.

The Emerging Qualities of the
Interactive-Relational Approach

The interactive-relational (I:R) approach emphasizes how the interviewer effects a deeper understanding of the interviewee through five factors:

- self-awareness
- authenticity
- attunement
- personal characteristics
- new relationship

How have elements of the I:R approach strengthened this interview?

> **Self-Awareness**
> - access to interviewer's feelings, disposition
> - self-knowledge
> - differentiating needs, motives, perspectives

First, the interviewer possessed *self-awareness,* the importance of the interviewer's *access to his or her feelings and disposition.* Although some traditional models of interviewing emphasize objectivity or minimize the interviewer's personal feelings, the I:R approach includes the importance of the interviewer's self-awareness. The degree to which an interviewer knows him- or herself and can differentiate his or her needs, motives, and perspectives from those of the interviewee is essential to obtain an inner view. Out of the fear of role confusion or countertransference (how the interviewer is personally affected by the interviewee), some may argue that such qualities of the interviewer pollute the interview. Some may feel that when the interviewer incorporates personal characteristics, the dynamics of the interaction result in either a casual, unproductive conversation; a breakdown of essential boundaries; or an invitation for unprofessional exchange.

In the case of Randy, I was in check with how my experience and feelings affected our exchange and confirmed my recommendations within the rules of the prison system. Awareness and resolution of my own feelings led me to how I would intervene. Negotiating my concerns within this system, I forestalled Randy's move to a maximum security prison and helped him become aware of his emotions. Ultimately, we shared an authentic exchange.

> **Authenticity**
> - recognizing values, beliefs, convictions
> - openness
> - monitoring roles, professionalism, genuine communication

Second, the interviewer reacted with *authenticity,* genuinely *recognizing his or her values, beliefs, and convictions. Openness* refers to the degree to which the interviewer provides access of oneself to the interviewee. Authenticity conveys one's personal investment without digressing to unrelated rumination. The I:R interviewer *monitors* authenticity through attentiveness to *roles, professionalism,* and a fundamental concern for how *genuine communication* affects the interviewee and the interview.

   In this experience with Randy, I authentically shared my experiences yet limited explicit examples of self-disclosure. For instance, I did not find it necessary to inform Randy of my father's death. However, as a result of my father's death, I felt a heightened sensitivity to his grief. I could vividly recall an emptiness and vulnerability. Although not explicit, Randy felt the force of my personal situation and identified the implicit manifestations of my attunement. I would hope not to project my feelings onto Randy, yet I was attuned to his feelings. Taking a risk, such as sitting away from the panic button, anticipating the impact of his loss, and intervening with the superintendent were authentic personal choices. Randy told me that he could "talk to" me but resented his counsel from the superintendent. My availability and support were qualitatively different from what he found with the superintendent. One might ask, Why was the superintendent received so poorly? Randy recalled that the superintendent had made reference to the fact that he read a book about death that emphasized the importance of crying to express feelings of loss. However genuine the intentions, the superintendent's advice did not convey his personal investment or support. His counsel did not effectively convey his own feelings (coming out of self-awareness) and his risk to attend and to extend.

Attunement
- attending
- extending

   Third, the interviewer *attuned,* attended and extended, to the interviewee while maintaining professional boundaries. Interviews that lack attunement often provide interviews that lack depth. In fact, lifeless interviews arise from those situations when interviewers merely complete forms or adhere to formalized guidelines. Although forms may provide the template for interviews, the interviewer needs to go beyond the answer and explore the context, situation, and experience of the interviewee because these may be just as important, often more important, than one's answer to a question. An interviewer raises a question and permits the interviewee to develop a response by *attending,* expressing care and concern through empathic techniques of verbal and nonverbal expression that convey interest in the person. In this way, the interviewer learns significant information about the interviewee's nature, choices, values, and life. Following the lead of the interviewee, by *extending,* the interviewer goes beyond the plan and allows the interviewee to participate actively in the process of genuine communication. Extending includes responsiveness to the interviewee in both word and action. Through attending and extending, the interviewer may increase the interviewee's desire to say more about him- or herself.

Upon meeting Randy, I asked him how he was managing. This open-ended question could have brought our work in several directions. He could have acted out and confirmed the apprehension of my colleagues. He could have been noncommunicative and kept the doors of his very active inner self closed. By attending to his thoughts, feelings, and needs, however, he felt that I cared about him. Here, attending did not guarantee that he would or could disclose his feelings; rather, it offered him the opportunity to express himself *vis-à-vis* my support. His loss of his father resonated within me. Randy's awareness of my care and concern enabled him to share his poems. It may very well be that our shared experience, the loss of a father, enabled me to attend more substantially through empathic response, gestures, and openness. In this particular story, there are several illustrations of attending and extending one's self as interviewer—from providing a safe, trusting setting to appealing to the superintendent not to transfer Randy. Often, one finds that such attendings and extendings invite reciprocity; more important, however, the interviewer must initiate the dynamic, the process of a deep and genuine connectedness, and maintain appropriate boundaries. Here, extending did not mean following him on some unrelated discussion; it meant carefully responding to his concerns in concrete ways.

Personal Characteristics
- individual characteristics shared
- characteristics enhance, resonate

Fourth, the interviewer incorporated *personal characteristics* into the interview. Whereas other techniques may overlook, suppress, or trivialize this fact (Brady, 1976; McCracken, 1988), this approach requires that the interviewer integrate his or her *characteristics* and recognize how they *enhance, resonate,* and affect the interviewee. The genuine expression of the interviewer's characteristics provides the foundation for an authentic exchange.

In the case of Randy, he had protected himself from his feelings and from sharing his innermost thoughts. What occurred in this interview that permitted him to show another very developed, yet private side? By his own description, what "impressed" him was his observation and experience of my trust.

Although I would have identified my demonstrated characteristics in the interview as risk-taking, openness, and nurturance, in addition to trust, what stood out for him was my willingness to treat (trust) him as a person and not as a prisoner.

New Relationship
- new shared space
- exploring one's history
- exploring one's motives

Fifth, the interviewer expressed support and action in the context of the *new relationship* between the interviewer and interviewee. Certainly, the spectrum of interviews does not usually invite the possibility for action, support, or placing one's self at risk, as in this account. The new relationship, however, offers one an opportunity to ascertain information from a *new shared space* for a fuller appreciation of "the facts." A huge difference exists between a nurse interviewing a patient with the intention of gathering a history, where, on one hand, he or she checks a list of true or false responses and, on the other hand, invites the patient to describe his or her experience of the problem, ascertaining information about the person and the context. A nurse primarily concerned with the facts of the physical well-being of a patient may learn more about both the emotional and physical health by engaging a patient in an I:R frame, of the new relationship, where the experience of one's *history* and *emotional state* is explored.

One's personal involvement plays a critical role in the interview process. An interviewer needs to maintain roles, to integrate the self into the process (see Chapter 3) as well as to check and recognize countertransference and personal issues (see Chapter 6). This allows for the conversational nature of the approach and the integration of interactive and relational elements. In the I:R approach, self-awareness, authenticity, attunement, personal characteristics, and the new relationship facilitate the interviewer in maintaining healthy parameters in service of the interviewee.

Interaction and Relationship

The integrity of the I:R approach derives from the *interaction* of individuals communicating on the basis of what they share in their *relationship* through their roles. To understand how the *process* of interviewing affects the *content* of the interview, an interviewer must first recognize the elements that comprise the two parts of this approach.

Interaction

The concept of *interaction* stems from the dynamics and role that the interviewer establishes.

The interaction includes
- Posturing
- Engagement
- Collaboration toward a balance of power
- Interviewer's stance
  - Observational self
  - Awareness of transference and countertransference
- New space toward a new relationship

The interaction addresses the particular ways in which dynamics of communication evolve between the interviewer and the interviewee. Interviewers approach interviewing differently based on how they understand themselves and their roles. The interaction in I:R involves five aspects regardless of the approach or difference among interviewers: (a) posture; (b) engagement; (c) collaboration toward a balance of power; (d) the interviewer's stance, with attention to observational self and awareness of transference and countertransference; and (e) the new space toward a new relationship.

The *posturing* of the interviewer and interviewee determines the course of an interview. It is dependent on the direction in communication, allocation of power, and definition of the roles of the participants (see Chapter 4).

Engagement describes the contact or range in potential areas of exploration permitted in an interaction. Specific posturing and relational styles help to establish the degree and quality of engagement.

Collaboration toward a balance of power acknowledges that either an interviewer or interviewee may establish power in or control an interview. Recognition and collaboration or balancing of power affect the quality of the interaction.

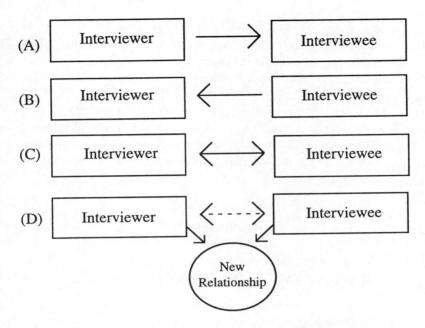

Figure 1.1. Development of the New Space Toward a New Relationship

Interviewer's stance refers to the fact that an interaction can be enhanced by the interviewer's awareness of an observational self, where the interviewer oversees the dynamics in communication in which he or she participates with the interviewee, on one hand, and actively engages in the interview, on the other. The interviewer's stance may facilitate the interaction through monitoring and management of transference and countertransference material.

The new stance toward a new relationship identifies the way in which participants move from their own point of view toward a shared perspective. The interaction of the participants may move in various directions, reflecting different control in the interview, where participants (A, B, C) are not *with* one another but communicate *at* or *to* one another. It may present the interviewer holding control (A), the interviewee directing the interviewer (B), or shared control, where direction emerges from both participants (C). Although acknowledging the shared control and direction of communication (dotted line), the new relationship (D) results when both participants essentially enter a new space, engaging collaboratively in a reciprocal manner.

The new space creates the setting for a new relationship in which attention on the "we" emerges in distinction from a focus on the "me" of the interviewer or the "you" of the interviewee.

Winnicott (1971) makes a claim for an important aspect of human life that he calls "experiencing." This is an intermediate area between self and other to which both the inner psychic reality (self) and the external environment (other) contribute. Often, interviews focus on the "you" (interviewee) or the "me" (interviewer), whereas the I:R approach emphasizes a collaborative stance that provides the foundation to incorporate fully the relational elements of the I:R approach.

Relationship

The *relationship* emerges in part from the interaction and evolves from reciprocation built on the quality of connectedness of the participants.

The relationship includes
- professional and personal alliance
- reciprocal engagement
- person orientation

The relationship results when the interviewer and interviewee leave their own perspectives and progress toward shared considerations. This relationship includes (a) professional and personal alliance, (b) reciprocal engagement, and (c) person orientation.

Professional and personal alliance qualifies the relationship as holding primary responsibilities to professional goals while engaging the personal qualities and alliance of the participants.

Reciprocal engagement refers to the deeper relationship that emerges because both participants express their thoughts, feelings, and beliefs to one another.

Person orientation conveys the quality of attunement to one another in which the participants act, demonstrating awareness, respect, and engagement of each other in ways that affirm the person while addressing the specific concern.

Legend:
E = Interviewee
R = Interviewer
• = Issue
O = Sphere of influence

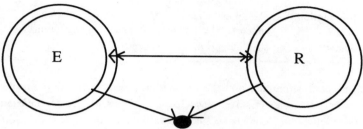

Figure 1.2. The I:R Approach

Within this purview, the interviewer maintains the professional tasks, purposes, and responsibilities with respect to the goals of the interview. The interviewer sets a personable tone in an interview by drawing on personal qualities and appropriate self-disclosure. Based on the interviewer's self-awareness, authenticity, and attunement and the interviewee's responsiveness, reciprocal engagement occurs. As the parties experience and explore such components of the relationship, the interview attains its potential. By developing both personal and professional dimensions in the new relationship, the participants may unravel defenses, present more of themselves, and even experience the opportunity for growth.

Potential for Action in the I:R Interview

The *potential for action* is the building block of the I:R approach. It refers to opportunities, or moments, in an interview that present themselves through exchanges where positive reciprocal sharing can lead to greater understanding and connectedness and can enhance communication (see Figure 1.2).

Qualities that **initiate** the **potential for action:**

- **characteristics**   an overlap or common points of reference drawn
                         from individual traits
- **experiences**   common points of reference for life events or
                         beliefs; distinct points of reference that, when
                         shared, result in the desire to explore
- **confirmation**   obtaining the feeling of being understood or
                         supported, leading to a willingness to engage further
- **interest**   shared motivation to engage

Such moments strengthen both the interaction and the relationship. The more an interviewer or interviewee seizes on such opportunities, the greater the chance to experience relational elements and the deeper the relationship can develop.

One can draw the analogy between the potential for action and the action potential regarding neurons, where the firing of neurons depends on particular electrochemical properties. Neurotransmitters (analogous to characteristics that affect communication) may assist in the firing of neurons to achieve communication between neurons (analogous to growth in understanding). However, some neurotransmitters (analogous to characteristics that may negatively affect communication) inhibit, retard, or prevent effective communication. The potential for action depends on the properties or the dynamics of the two personalities. The compatibility (of characteristics) of the interviewer and interviewee determines whether they will "be fired" and resonate. Therefore, individual characteristics of the participants have the potential for facilitating the continuously deepening, growing, and revealing process needed for the interview—or may simply misfire, ending that potential. The potential for action parallels the firing of neurons in the analogy because it, in effect, waits to see if excitation or inhibition of a message will occur.

In this creative setting, both people present themselves. A deepening of an interview likely occurs when both participants share, appreciate, and experience each other's characteristics.

Components of the **potential for action:**

- **vulnerability**   a willingness to discover if mutual interest exists
                      and if there exists a desire to enter a personal
                      process
- **response**   an acknowledgment of the presence of mutually
                      shared or appreciated characteristics
- **action**   the motivation to nurture and to fuel the encounter

---

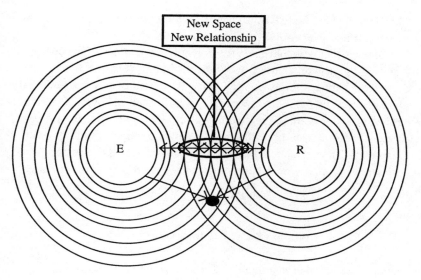

Figure 1.3.

The new relationship provides a setting where authentic dialogue can occur: where stories of one's past reflect new understandings that develop as a result of this present interviewing experience. The potential for action leads to the beginning of the new relationship, a new beginning for the interviewer and interviewee.

Process of the Potential for Action

Figure 1.3 illustrates the I:R process of a discussion of a particular topic between the interviewer and interviewee. A dialogue that includes positive reciprocal sharing creates a larger consciousness. It shows that a wider awareness, indicated by the larger concentric circle, results from the successful positive realization of the potential for action. The model illustrates two results: First, from the interaction, a relationship likely evolves as the participants draw closer to one another when the points of reference built by successful expression of the potential for action (more concentric circles or spheres of influence) increase; second, through the relationship, a deeper understanding likely evolves as points of reference and sharing of experiences increase the chances to relate authentically and attune mutually.

The relationship, fueled by the *potential for action,* depends on the engagement of the two people.

The process that develops from the potential for action reveals continuously expanding growth, sharing, and understanding (as shown by the concentric circles) between the two individuals. To a great extent, the potential for action depends on the interviewer's willingness to be spontaneous and to share relevant material (thoughts, feelings) from his or her life. In this way, the I:R model contrasts starkly with static, traditional models of interviewing (see Chapter 4). Thus, this model shows how the interaction and relationship and, ultimately, the interview continuously evolve according to the resourcefulness of the participants.

Components of I:R Interviewing

The components that distinguish I:R from casual conversation or traditional interviewing follow:

Components of the I:R Approach
- an I:R way of thinking
- the role of the person of the interviewer
- the collaboration of people
- the orientation to the present
- the potential for action
- the energizing pulse

AN I:R WAY OF THINKING

An I:R way of thinking presumes that the interviewer understands the significance of his or her position and has clarity about his or her purpose. This way of thinking distinguishes how an interviewer can best understand the interviewee through the elements associated with interaction and relationship. This affirms the necessity of the interviewer's self-awareness, engaging in authentic dialogue, and attuning to another's circumstance. I:R thought prescribes a model for interviewing based on the development of relational and integrative thought and interdisciplinary scholarship.

ROLE OF THE PERSON OF THE INTERVIEWER

In the I:R approach, the interviewer implements personal attributes and values that he or she brings to the interview. One's personal commitments and values have a significant effect on the interview and provide an essential resource for deepening the encounter. Although people often veil their personal qualities and beliefs, these individual aspects influence the interview. Rather than relegating the role of the interviewer by indoctrination to the confines of a particular interviewing technique or traditional system, the interviewer appropriately expresses him- or herself and avoids masking personal views that may be encouraged by the so-called value-free approach. Through such actions in his or her role, the interviewer invites the interviewee to reciprocate.

COLLABORATION OF PEOPLE

In I:R, the collaboration of people occurs in the interaction and the relationship. Through interaction, the participants collaborate to form the basis for establishing a relationship. In the relationship, collaboration yields reciprocity and greater understanding. When the interviewer acts in an open manner, the interviewee can model the interviewer's behavior and a collaboration may develop.

ORIENTATION TO THE PRESENT

Whereas most interviews focus on past events, the I:R interview concentrates on the present moment. With an attentive eye to the active present, this interview method provides clarity about both the past and the present. In this present state of thinking, growing, sharing, and revealing, the participants may investigate an incident from the past resulting in spontaneous, new insight in contrast to recounted facts. The interviewer experiences a more authentic and direct encounter of the interviewee, bringing about an understanding of the interviewee's current values, beliefs, and qualities. This affirms the positive alliance with the interviewee.

POTENTIAL FOR ACTION

The potential for action identifies the opportunities in an encounter where the two people move toward a shared experience. The experiences that emerge will help create the new space (new relationship) and increase understanding of the interviewee. When the participants experience and share their lives, careful listening by the interviewer may transform the retelling of an event into an occasion for sharing and growth. This action, initiated by either the interviewer or interviewee, may follow up on the personal thoughts and feelings of both. For example, interviews often begin with reflections of old stories. Such reflections bring the opportunity to participate in the potential for action by creating a new interaction and relationship.

THE ENERGIZING PULSE

The energizing pulse defines the initial moment where resonance of characteristics or feelings occurs following the potential for action that draws the participants into the new relationship. This moment and this experience indicates the connectedness of the participants where they share the spark of life in an effective interview. Enhancement of the connectedness in this new relationship is seminal to the I:R approach. This process entails much more than empathy or alliance. Moreover, we cannot reduce to or produce through mechanical techniques, the critical—yet elusive—nature of what occurs in the interaction and relationship. I:R results from a communion of people.

A movement toward integration of the self and a relational stance has evolved in several fields of study. The next chapter examines interviewing practices in view of this orientation and compares them with the interactive-relational approach.

2

Placing the Interactive-Relational Approach in Context

After summarizing the objectives of the interactive-relational approach (I:R), this chapter compares the I:R perspective with traditional approaches for interviewing. In addition, this discussion examines the influence, contributions, and distinctions of the I:R approach with similar relational perspectives in interdisciplinary studies: psychoanalysis and relational psychology, perception and epistemology, translation and dialogue, and women's studies. Finally, we address themes in relational interviewing that we associate with this interviewing technique.

The I:R Approach

Legend:
E = Interviewee   • = Issue
R = Interviewer   O = Sphere of influence

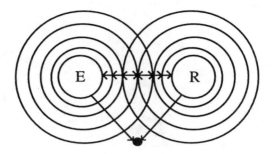

Figure 2.1.

The I:R approach emphasizes the importance of the growing interaction and relationship between interviewer and interviewee. Figure 2.1 shows that as the participants communicate on a given topic, they also engage interpersonally. This approach argues that an interview best achieves its intentions through mutual engagement of both the interviewee and the interviewer.

Whereas an interview usually begins with a specific purpose, an *interaction* evolves within the I:R approach that allows for and encourages an exchange of thoughts, beliefs, and emotions. Furthermore, the interviewer and the interviewee develop a *relationship* that enhances deeper awareness of each other and themselves. The success of this approach results from the interviewer drawing on personal characteristics that serve as resources and the foundation for identification, revelation, and understanding of the interviewee. As the participants engage each other, their sharing deepens, interactions increase, and the relationship builds, as portrayed by their overlapping spheres of influence in Figure 2.1.

Comparison With Traditional
Approaches to Interviewing

Many psychological concerns (i.e., the histories, thoughts, beliefs, drives, and concerns of both the interviewer and the interviewee) enhance the I:R approach. Because I:R contains similar elements addressed by different psychological perspectives, it is helpful to place this approach in the context of the major schools of psychology.

Classical psychoanalysis requires the interviewer to maintain an observational posture in his or her relationship to the interviewee (Giovacchini, 1972; Mollon, 1986). Although the inferred objective distance facilitates insight concerning one's intrapsychic process, it inhibits the relational dimension that takes place between the participants in the I:R approach.

Traditional behavioral psychology's experimental design reduces the interviewer's role to scientific architect and the interviewee's role to that of "subject" (Cooper, Heron, & Heword, 1987). This perspective does not take into consideration significant relational components critical to advancing an interview.

Humanistic psychology affirms the positive nature of the person in the process of growth. Although the I:R approach finds agreement with this value, I:R moves significantly beyond existential approaches by exploring the particular relational dynamics developed between the interviewer and interviewee.

We observe that the three classical forces in psychology remain confined by the foci of their particular theorists. For example, in humanistic psychology, Rogerian theory advises one to express "unconditional, positive regard" (Rogers, 1980, p. 116) for the client (the interviewee). Carl Rogers advocated "genuineness, realness, or congruence" (p. 116) and an empathic relationship, concepts embodied by the I:R approach. Such "unconditional, positive regard" (Holdstock & Rogers, 1977) and "genuineness," however, may result in a paradox. Because an interviewer may not always possess unconditional, positive regard, Rogers's stance may create a dynamic that does not provide for authentic communication, perhaps leading to artificial and formulaic interviews. The I:R technique bases the process on the participant's characteristics, authentic exchange, and the resources that the two people bring to the interview. As in Rogers's person-centered theory, the integrity of the I:R approach is derived from the authentic interaction of individuals communicating with their whole being—on the basis of what they bring to the relationship and what they experience with one another.

When a method identifies or requires singular traits of the interviewer, he or she may be led to feign such qualities and may contradict the aim of an authentic exchange. For this reason, in I:R, the interviewer is guided to recognize his or her personal characteristics and to integrate his or her qualities.

Interdisciplinary Perspectives

Specialists in related fields of interviewing have expressed dissatisfaction with the limitations brought about by traditional approaches to understanding human lives. Although the central elements in the I:R approach have not been the focal points of others, writers in four interdisciplinary fields express similar concerns about the inadequacy of addressing human lives through traditional approaches: (a) contributors to the fields of psychoanalysis and relational psychology, (b) writers about perception and epistemology, (c) scholars on translation and dialogue, and (d) authors concerned with the methodology of women's studies. Writers in these areas oppose the limitations inherent in traditional approaches to studying and understanding human lives. This section considers the contributive elements of their perspectives in view of the I:R approach.

PSYCHOANALYSIS AND RELATIONAL PSYCHOLOGY

Although classical psychoanalytic theory requires that a therapist maintain a professional distance when relating to the patient, contemporary writers in the field of psychoanalysis have criticized such views. For example, Kohut (1977) writes about the significance of the quality of interaction with the therapist, whereas others have described particular characteristics of the relationship that require attention in the therapeutic process (DeVoge & Beck, 1978; Ford, 1978; Mitchell, 1988). For example, the personality characteristics of the patient in relationship to the therapist have been supported in psychoanalytic literature (Schwartz, 1984). Beyond such openness concerning the contributions of these writers, Wolf (1983) discussed the therapeutic efforts of "self-revelations."

Shifts in psychoanalytic theory have opened the way and improved the climate for therapists and interviewers to explore the benefits of developing interpersonal communication between patient (interviewee) and therapist (interviewer). With greater awareness of the elements identified in the field of psychotherapy, interviewers can integrate themselves more actively into the I:R framework, attaining broader interviewing objectives.

Dave Mearns (Mearns & Thorne, 1988) defined a healthy therapeutic relationship in view of such sensitivities (here referring to the counselor that can equally relate to interviewer):

1. The counselor is open about his purpose.
2. The counselor is responsible to his client not for him.
3. The counselor does not manipulate his client but is prepared to be manipulated.
4. The counselor does not profess to know what is "good" for the client.
5. The counselor is not concerned about "success."
6. The counselor is clear about what he is willing to offer the client at every stage.
7. The counselor is committed to the client and will "fight" for the relationship.
8. The counselor is prepared to invest himself in the relationship.
9. The counselor desires the client's freedom to be himself. (pp. 28-34)

Although these guidelines are positive and helpful, they remain clinical, one-sided, and impersonal.

Because of such legitimate concerns as the fear of confusing roles, the ambiguity involved in defining a professional and personal relationship, and the problem of therapeutic boundaries, there continues to be reservation concerning the active involvement of the interviewer. As a result, such reservations limit the relationship and veil critical information, often obscuring the very essence of the subject matter.

Judy Kantrowitz (1986) points out that a critical and often overlooked aspect of the patient/analyst relationship is the complement of the analyst's personal qualities with those of the patient. Kantrowitz contends that the more the analyst can understand and remain aware of his or her contribution to the transference, the less likely it is that the analyst's personal limitations and personality adversely affect treatment. This observation applies in the interview experience as well: The interviewer can deepen the encounter by understanding and being aware of his or her impact by *identifying* and *using* his or her *personal resources and characteristics*.

By definition, personal characteristics are idiosyncratic. To a great extent, our approaches, turns, emphases, and foci in interviews may serve as transparencies of our identity and inner nature. Just as Freud's theory grappled with psychosexual forces, and Skinner's work examined the effect of environmental contigencies on daily life, our theories often project our personal preoccupations, bias, and vision. Similarly, the interviewer's *approach* may reflect the interviewer in terms of his or her values and commitments. In the final analysis, recognition of the human design(er) in an interview is crucial. This recognition identifies critical operative forces in an interview. In this way, the I:R approach acknowledges the personal factors often hidden behind formalism or professionalism. Once acknowledged, these elements can infuse the interview with life and allow it to develop.

PERCEPTION AND EPISTEMOLOGY

Patricia Carini (1979) approaches the study of human lives by challenging the maxim that "the scientific method is the path to valid knowledge and that it is a method equally applicable to all phenomena" (p. 1). For Carini, each person "is and remains" an ultimate mystery, and this sensitivity forms the foundation for her work.

Carini's work in perception and human development demonstrated her struggle to present the human person as a whole, integrated being through naturalistic observation and understanding. Her emphasis on the individual, however, goes beyond the measures of scientific inquiry. Carini emphasized that one's own transpersonal dimensions and quest require an approach to seeing the interviewee that expresses his or her journey for life's meaning. These concerns echo those of the I:R approach: "It is never so much the facts, circumstances, and literal occurrences that describe and portray the person as the *relationship* the person makes to these literal events, and the choices that follow from the mode of relating" (p. 28). Drawing on the physicist Niels Bohr's work, Carini acknowledged that the perceiver (in effect, the interviewer) "when searching for harmony in life . . . must never forget that in the drama of existence we are ourselves both players and spectators" (p. 14). Thus, Carini saw the dual role of the interviewer as both active and "affecting" an experience.

Carini's position on the observer's relationship is similar to the intrapsychic sharing emphasized in the I:R approach. Whereas Carini wants the work in human perception and development to address the recurrent events of one's life, the I:R approach sees the interview itself as participating in the relationship of the events of another person's life and, as an event, participating in life itself.

Carini's perspective, like the I:R approach, proposed that one give attention to the observer's vision, for which one must account. Carini suggested that acknowledging this aspect of the interaction makes the presentation of one's life accurate and vital. The I:R approach explains how qualities result in the active participation of the interviewer with the interviewee. Whereas this perspective created "mutual viewing" for Carini, the I:R approach facilitates understanding of both the interviewee and oneself as interviewer.

Anthony Barrand (1988) observed that we reduce meaning to techniques that can recreate a particular experience. He explained that participation in the process of understanding meaning brings one to an experience quite different from what an examination of the sum of the parts allows: "Beauty and meaning lie not in having all the parts . . . but in how they relate to each other" (pp. 27, 31). In a similar way, Carini stated that meaning is not a thing, an object, or an entity itself. Rather, the word *meaning* designates the experience of a relationship that enhances and makes more vivid both the events and the people it joins.

Holstein and Gubrium (1995) explain that both parties in an interview are necessarily and unavoidably "active. Each is involved in meaning-making work" (p. 4). They explain that meaning is elicited not just through sharp questioning and conveyed by replies; through the interview experience, it is actively and communicatively assembled. As with I:R, this perspective presents the interviewees not as repositories of knowledge who are to be explored and excavated (and sometimes pillaged), but rather as constructors of knowledge with the interviewers. Holstein and Gubrium continue that when the interview is understood as a dynamic, meaning-making occasion, different criteria apply from a traditional, scientific interview that evaluates in terms of *reliability*—the extent to which the same results emerge from a situation—and *validity*—the extent to which an inquiry finds the true answer. Their model of "active interviewing" is defined as an interpretive practice involving respondent and interviewer in an ongoing process of interpreting "structures, resources and orientation" (p. 16). Their discussion, however, is conceptual rather than a demonstration of how one constructs such interviews.

The vision of Carini (1979), the "meaning" in Barrand's (1988) terminology, and the "meaning-making" of Holstein and Gubrium (1995) find a natural foil in the I:R approach because it expresses the importance of one's participation in the process of interaction and relationship. In the I:R approach, the interviewer and interviewee invite and experience vulnerability, sharing, growth, and understanding.

Carini clarified what *opportunity* means through her discussion of imagination. She explained that imagination is possible through "immersion in the object of study through time" and through awareness of its "polarities which describe its coherence (unity) and its duality (transformation)" (Carini, 1979,

p. 19). Carini described the observation as "a quest, a searching." The I:R approach parallels this quest in that the interviewer seeks more than answers to interesting questions; the interviewer becomes a seeker of understanding. The discussion of the I:R approach remains consistent with Carini's attitude concerning how an interviewer raises questions not in the interest of abstract analysis but as a means and an opportunity of entering into the interviewee's boundaries: "to enter there, and to dwell there" (Carini, 1979, p. 20). In this way, a sharing emerges as the interviewer's own being resonates with the interviewee's experience.

TRANSLATION AND DIALOGUE

Dennis Tedlock (1985) advocated that one should convey the experience of a story not only by narration but also by a method that reenacts the encounter. His work aligns with the I:R approach in that it focuses on participating in the event in the present encounter, not only repeating what has already been said but also enabling the reader to participate in the dialogue as it occurred.

Through his concept of the "audible text," Tedlock presents translation ("analogical tradition") as dialogue ("dialogical anthropology") (Tedlock, 1988). Tedlock's approach to interpretation expresses the thoughts of the interpreter at the same time he presents the story. This active participation by the interpreter parallels the I:R approach that characterizes the role of the interviewer as participant and explains the relationship of the interviewer to the interviewee. In addition, the interviewer shares his or her internal association through the interviewer's personal thoughts and feelings in the transcription. In this way, the reader has a fuller awareness of the workings of the interview and the encounter of the interviewer and interviewee.

This approach to the dialogue provides a more active position for the reader of the interview, allowing the reader deeper insight into what occurred in the interview process through the means of the interviewer's annotation. Tedlock's approach is used in the two chapters presenting interviews with Lucille Ball and B. F. Skinner. In examining this adaptation of Tedlock's presentation of "dialogue," the reader participates in the process and variables affecting the critical turns of the I:R interview. As used in this book, Tedlock's concept is developed by annotating the transcription in a manner that conveys the interviewer's experience, thoughts, and feelings.

J. D. Douglas (see Holstein & Gubrium, 1995) presents the subject of "creative interviewing," which focuses on the role of the interviewer, to explore the "deep experiences" of respondents. By exploring the "emotional wellsprings" of interviewees, Douglas states that one "gets to know the real subject behind the respondent" and accesses "deep disclosure." Similar to collaborative aspects of I:R, Douglas explains creative interviewing as "partially the product of creative interactions—of mutual searches for understanding, of soul communication" (p. 13).

WOMEN'S STUDIES

The I:R approach addresses several of the concerns about the special or alternative methodology required for interviewing women. Many feminist writers agree that one should interview women and men differently (Gilligan, 1982; Miller, 1976; Reinharz, 1992). They point out that male-oriented perspectives dominate psychoanalytic and mechanical interviews. They argue that this male stance misses critical dimensions of the interviewing process. The I:R approach holds that the analytic, mechanical, and scientific approaches, although helpful, generally limit interviewing methodology. I:R shows that the relational dimension is equally vital in the interviewing of both men and women.

Ann Oakley (1981), in her review article on feminist methodology, observes three fundamental yet detrimental practices in traditional approaches to interviewing: First, it is a one-way process in which the interviewer elicits and receives but does not give information; second, the interviewer casts interviewees in a role that is "narrow and objectified"; and third, such interviews do not attend to the personal dimension present in social interaction (Oakley, 1981, p. 30). Oakley's comments remain consistent with a basic principle of feminist studies that aims at validating women's subjective experiences. In agreement, the I:R approach considers subjective experience as part of a more comprehensive report.

Some of the significant areas shared between women's studies research and the I:R approach include (a) the social and personal characteristics of the interviewer, (b) the interviewee's feelings about being interviewed and about the interview, (c) the interviewer's feelings about his or her interviewees, (d) the quality of the interviewer-interviewee interaction, (e) the hospitality offered by interviewees to interviewers, (f) the attempts by interviewers to use interviewees as sources of information, and (g) the extension of interviewer-interviewee encounters into more broadly based social relationships.

Oakley argued against traditional interviewing approaches, first, because the "use of prescribed interviewing is morally indefensible"; second, because of "general and irreconcilable contradictions at the heart of textbook paradigm(s)"; and third, because "interviewing is best achieved when the relationship of interviewer and interviewee is non-hierarchical and when the interviewer inserts his or her own personal identity in the relationship" (Oakley, 1981, p. 61). Her third point emphasized the fact that the relationship is a joint collaborative enterprise in counterdistinction to the subject/observer paradigm.

Women's studies emphasize the importance of narratives that respect the integrity of a woman's life and avoid the evaluative categories (often considered as "male") that limit the understanding of the person. Here we see a distinction between biography, presented through the author's eyes, and autobiography, which often lacks objectivity with the recommended nonevaluated narratives (Personal Narratives Group, 1989).

Researchers in women's studies express suspicion about the traditional scholar's assumptions regarding interpretations of life stories (Eichenbaum & Orbach, 1982; Gilligan, 1982). Feminist writers acknowledge the interpreter's involvement in the process of creating a personal narrative through a relationship. This relationship reflects the individuality of both narrator and interpreter and differs in each interviewing situation. Feminist relational theory emphasizes that the self is typically portrayed as existing in "space, characterized by the 'possession' of various unique attributes . . . demarcated or bounded in some way . . . and interacting from a place of separation or containment" (Jordan, 1991, p. 142). They criticize the focus on *boundary,* which emphasizes *protecting* and *defining* rather than *meeting* or *communicating.* The I:R approach extends this thinking to a more moderate position (similarly adapted by Chirban, 1993). The interview (new space) serves as the place for *meeting* and *communicating* while, as a result of the I:R experience, the individual has the opportunity to feel strengthened *with* boundaries that serve to protect and define oneself further.

The I:R approach treats the roles of the interviewer and interviewee as neither hierarchical nor equal, although these two individuals have, of course, different roles. Growth, understanding, and transformation may develop from collaboration.

Themes in Relational Interviewing

The I:R approach to interviewing has evolved out of or been influenced by the aforementioned studies. The following concepts and techniques used in interviewing invite discussion that one may associate with I:R.

EMPATHY

Empathy is the capacity to understand another's feelings or ideas. The empathic quality is a powerful bond that enables one to identify with another (Gladstein et al., 1987). Empathy, a recognized and standard characteristic of the interviewing process (Feiner & Kiersky, 1994; Friend & Cook, 1992; Morrison, 1995; Zima, 1983), has found its way into the doctrines of interviewing theory and has been identified as a basic tool. In a review article, C. H. Patterson (1994) concluded, "There are few things in the field of psychology for which the evidence is so strong. The evidence for the necessity, if not the sufficiency, of the therapist conditions of accurate empathy, respect, warmth and therapeutic genuineness is incontrovertible" (p. 437). The I:R approach values empathy as well as several other qualities of effective interviewing (e.g., listening skills, openness, respectfulness, and care). However, I:R places greater emphasis on how one's characteristics, both innate and developed, affect an interview.

Probably more than any characteristic, researchers acknowledge empathy as essential for an interview and have developed and defined numerous teachable, though often mechanical, approaches and techniques for training interviewers to be empathic. To some extent, the principle of empathy may hold in traditional interviewing the role of the critical components of a relationship as considered in I:R.

As stated earlier, the classic psychoanalytic position concerning the interaction of interviewer with the interviewee requires neutrality and non-partiality. When personal aspects of the interviewer enter into the interaction, concern arises that the interviewer may jeopardize credibility and clarity of the roles. Reflecting sensitivity to this subject, one author advises that a healthy friendship is one held by two equals, while a healthy counseling relationship is one of unequals; psychotherapists are neutral advocates, but friends are emotionally biased advocates (Katz, 1963).

Carl Rogers's approach concerning empathy is often presented as a teachable characteristic. Probably for Rogers himself, empathy was an authentic personal quality. But if one is not empathic by nature, should one nevertheless feign empathy? If a counselor plays this "empathic role," would such behavior undercut Rogers's basic premise of "genuineness"? Rogers also defined empathy as nonevaluative, unconditional, and nonjudgmental. Might it not be relational, interactive, genuine, and ultimately helpful to act in an evaluative and conditional manner? An interviewer feigning empathy may cause the interviewee to feel encouraged but possibly as an object of a one-way, unnatural, unauthentic interaction that ultimately may reveal its inconsistency and limit the depth of the interview. From my perspective, empathy is valuable when it is genuinely expressed. The degree to which one may marshal caring qualities and awaken one's dormant attentive qualities for interviewing would be encouraged with I:R as invaluable.

Carl Rogers observed that the more experienced the therapist, the more empathic the therapist. The more effective and experienced therapist exhibits more empathic gestures. However, one may conjecture that the more experienced interviewer becomes more relational based on his or her own qualities. With experience, one learns that the relational element often works. I believe that many describe the concept of empathy to address the relational dimensions.

Ultimately, teaching empathy may defeat the desired result. If empathy conveys a quality in the interaction that may be foreign to the relationship or to the interviewer, feigned empathy may prove detrimental. In the I:R approach, empathy deepens an interview not when it is manufactured or even learned but, more fundamentally, when it is experienced as genuine. Such empathy promotes the relationship and deepens the experience of understanding felt by the interviewee.

LISTENING

Good listening skills improve the discussion in a relationship and move the participants away from static roles. Devices such as "intentional" interviewing, attention to verbal and nonverbal responses, and direct communication about issues may expand the interview to more than a supportive environment for observation to one in which the interviewee feels encouraged to share (Underwood, 1984). The I:R approach to interviewing assumes a foundation of effective listening skills.

The active listening role enables an interviewer to appreciate a wide range of both subtle and apparent revealing parts in communication with an interviewee (Ivey, Ivey, & Browning, 1993). Formal notions about interviewing processes and theories that more generally guide the interviewer are often insufficient. Although effective listening skills may isolate helpful techniques, good listening skills are not enough. Interviewing skills alone may render an interview as a skeleton or collection of data. In the psychological literature, effective listening technique is found to encourage the interviewer:interviewee relationship, which deepens the encounter, understanding, and/or growth of an interviewee. For example, Robert Langs (1978), in *The Listening Process*, clarified how the therapist and analyst listen by examining therapeutic interactions of the cognitive dimensions, role, unique evocations, and interactional mechanisms.

Virginia Satir (Satir, Stachowick, & Taschman, 1980) explained how effective listening requires that the participants in an interview enter the frame of reference for "the moment." She explained that when the listener constructs meaning through checking with the sender to ensure accuracy and understanding, one may be totally engaged: "All of me is geared to you, and I feel this totally in my body. It is a lifting feeling" (p. 157). She advised that such listening produces connectedness when we realize (a) that we are dealing with another human being with rich experiences, and (b) that we must teach each other how to understand. Such listening is presented in I:R as creating a deeper engagement. Through the resonation of mutual listening, one progresses toward deeper understanding.

THERAPEUTIC ALLIANCE

The term *therapeutic alliance* refers to the connection of interviewer and interviewee in therapy. The alliance or relational bond between client and therapist has been viewed as a barometer for treatment effectiveness (Safran, McMain, Crocker, & Murray, 1990). The interviewer's perceived characteristics often deepen the alliance with the interviewee. Traditionally, therapeutic alliances are often established as projections of the interviewee onto the interviewer, minimizing the actual personal qualities of the interviewer if not extinguishing them from the process (Weinberg, 1984). Terms contributed to the exchange, such as "professional" and "role," identify nondescript images of the interviewer reflecting the isolation or separateness of the interviewer from an interaction with the interviewee. Because a traditional understanding of the therapeutic alliance focuses on facilitating the therapeutic relationship with the interviewee, it does not often attend to the role of a real relationship with the interviewer.

Modern trends in the literature concerning the therapeutic alliance advocate that the therapist should treat each patient differently because each person is unique (Casement, 1991; Minuchin & Fishman, 1981). From the perspective of the I:R approach, each *interviewer* maintains his or her unique status. In this sense, the I:R approach expands the notion of the therapeutic alliance for interviewing. Here, the interviewer conveys genuine interest by seeking to engage shared qualities: care pulls for care, honesty pulls for honesty. Through direct interaction with the interviewer, who conveys openness and sharing, an interviewee experiences genuine qualities and is likewise encouraged to share and convey genuine feelings.

Notably, recent attitudes of clinical practitioners acknowledge that patient collaboration has advantages for the therapeutic alliance. This perspective focuses attention on how the therapist's personality, skill, and technique interact with the patient problems brought to psychotherapy (Colson et al., 1988).

Rather than perceiving personal feelings as obstacles (i.e., causing harm for the role that a patient holds with his or her therapist), the I:R approach suggests recognition and management (not suppression) of such feelings. In this way, the therapeutic alliance is a *working* alliance. The I:R approach points out that the frame of "professionalism" hampers the relationship for interviewing outside of therapy. When the interviewer assumes a false role, he or she denies or loses personhood. It follows that Carl Rogers conducted interviews effectively because he *was* Carl Rogers. By simply applying his response or qualities, at best, one interviews like Carl Rogers. This situation is avoided in the I:R approach by emphasizing that the interviewer be him- or herself and allow the resourcefulness and dynamism of that reality to facilitate the interview.

TRANSFERENCE

A healthy therapeutic alliance often resolves problems from a "positive transference," a projection of one of the interviewee's significant personal relationships onto the interviewer (Casement, 1991). Transference, however, does not reflect a genuine relationship between participants. Therefore, when an interviewer assumes a role by choice or through transference, rather than presenting the self, the genuine intervention is inhibited.

For Freud, cure emerged through the resolution of the transference, where the individual distinguished his or her history and feelings of projections from reality. Enabling a person to gain awareness of such unconscious activity is one of the most basic challenges of therapy. This transference not only projects onto the interviewer but superimposes the self (interviewee) onto the other (interviewer) (Weinberg, 1984). Traditional analytic literature concludes that growth is critical to the management of transference (Gill, 1989; Racker, 1987). Therefore, the interviewer becomes a tabula rasa and attends to the interviewee's reposition of his or her processes. Because an interviewer's personal interaction contaminates the process, one may have concern that a relationship between interviewer and interviewee that draws on their personal characteristics may prove counterproductive and untrue to the therapeutic task at hand.

Can the interviewer develop the wealth of information acquired through the projected relationship? Or can transference be developed even further from an actual relationship between the interviewer and the interviewee? Because the transferential relationship is a false relationship, could a genuine therapeutic relationship emerge? To the all-or-nothing option, Thomas Paolino (1982) offers an alternative for therapy that also applies to interviewing. Paolino contends that the relationship between analyst and patient operates in *four* dimensions: transference neurosis, therapeutic alliance, narcissistic alliance, and real relationship. Paolino argues that the analyst and patient must fully recognize and actually use each of these aspects. Distinctions such as these helpfully point out that the therapeutic encounter need not remain solely unidimensional and that pursuit of the relationship and interaction may prove appropriate in particular cases and develop on behalf of the therapeutic and interviewing goals. Additionally, Judy Kantrowitz (1986) observes that a critical element commonly overlooked in examining the nature of change in psychoanalysis is the match between patient and analyst. She suggests that the more the analyst can understand his or her contribution to the transference experience, the less likely personal limitations and the effect of one's personality will adversely affect treatment.

For the I:R approach, the interviewer is aided by awareness of the transference that he or she stirs. Movement beyond transference toward a genuine relationship is fostered through the process of the I:R approach, which engages understanding of the interviewee. The degree to which an interviewer may distinguish, explore, and move beyond the transference will provide significant understanding of the interviewee.

COUNTERTRANSFERENCE

Countertransference, or the feelings and thoughts of the therapist generated by the client or patient, traditionally has been viewed as material for
private assessment by the therapist, again reflecting aspects associated not as
genuine dimensions of the relationship between the patient and therapist but
as by-products of the therapist associations and projections. An article in the
American Psychological Association Monitor (DeAngelis, 1989) featured a
debate on this question. The article contrasted "conservative analysts," who
believe that self-disclosure is inevitably harmful, with therapists who view
the sharing of one's feelings with a client at times as a "crucial kind of
intervention" (p. 24).

Virginia Satir's work in family therapy reflects the spontaneous, bal-
anced, and relational orientation presented in I:R concerning countertransference (Satir et al., 1980). She acknowledged,

> There is no rule about this. . . . I might say, "You know, when you look like that
> it reminds me of when I was five . . . I was suddenly feeling very helpless."
> Sometimes this has helped clear the air. . . . When your therapy does not move,
> for the most part there is something holding back the flow. . . . I once had the
> governor of a state ask me to take a case. Though I was much too busy and didn't
> have the time, I took the case against my better judgment. For three interviews
> nothing happened. Then I got in touch with my narcissism, my feeling of "Oh,
> boy! The governor wants me!" . . . When I told the client about all that and got
> past it, then we could get to work. (pp. 149-150)

Family therapy requires the use of self. The spontaneous, unplanned,
discernment of an interviewer emerges as a basic tool in family therapy
(Bowen, 1978; Minuchin & Fishman, 1981). Therefore, Minuchin and Fishman
(1981) advised, "There are limitations on his use of self, determined by his
personal characteristics and the characteristics of the family" (p. 31). Attention to how the matching of personal characteristics facilitates effective
communication is addressed in I:R (see Chapter 3—"The Personal Characteristics of the Interviewer").

Hard-and-fast rules about countertransference should not direct how an
interviewer manages personal associations. In the I:R approach, one's self-
awareness, authenticity, and attunement (themes presented in Chapter 3)
become the guideposts for assessing and managing countertransference.

Theodore Reich describes the traditional counseling orientation as "wor-
shipping the bitch goddess objectivity." The article also identifies a moderate

position on this topic by therapists who would disclose their own views "on rare occasions, during a major therapeutic impasse or crisis." The so-called "radical therapists" would reveal their personal views "as an aspect of their interpretive repertoire on an ongoing basis" (DeAngelis, 1989, p. 24). Furthermore, from his book *Understanding Countertransference: From Projective Identification to Empathy,* Michael Tansey (1989) indicates that countertransference "can be a gold mine of information on understanding, and can lay the groundwork for interpretations that can really make a difference" (p. 3).

In the final analysis, countertransference need not interfere with a relationship between interviewer and interviewee. A preferred alternative exists to the traditional position that emotional distance seems the most effective approach to therapeutic interaction. A relational posture could provide more productive and more genuine opportunities for growth that assist in understanding the person.

SELF-DISCLOSURE

One intervention that writers have suggested contributes to the relational dimension in psychotherapy is *self-disclosure.* In personal relationships, self-disclosure—revealing one's self, history, or personal information—creates the environment for mutual understandings (Derlega, Matts, Petronio, & Margulis, 1993). The impact of self-disclosure in professional settings continues to be carefully researched as a means of generating a facilitative atmosphere and enhancing communication (Giannandrea & Murphy, 1973; Goldstein, 1994; Nilsson, Strassberg, & Bannon, 1979; Peca-Baker & Friedlander, 1989; VandeCreek & Angstadt, 1985).

Several investigations have indicated that a counselor's self-disclosures tend to enhance the client's attraction to the counselor (Klein & Friedlander, 1987; cf. Hoffman-Graff, 1977; Murphy & Scasz, 1972; Nilsson et al., 1979). Such studies show that the counselor's disclosures reflect similarity to or agreement with the client (Klein & Friedlander, 1987; Giannandrea & Murphy, 1973; Mann & Murphy, 1975; Nilsson et al., 1979). Studies have shown that subjects rating counselors across a variety of professional (e.g., competency) and personal (e.g., likability) dimensions evaluated significantly more favorably disclosing counselors over counselors who do not self-disclose (Nilsson et al., 1979). However, researchers have been unclear about which components most enhance the relationship—from examining the act of revealing personal information to the information itself. Both the disclosure and the similarity of information had a considerably positive impact on the client's experience during the counseling session (Peca-Baker & Friedlander, 1989). The I:R approach, as with contemporary advances in psychoanalytic theory and relational psychology, has at its core the authentic dimensions of positive alliances. This encourages the interviewer's and the interviewee's self-awareness and mutual understanding.

In recent years, the move to develop "the relational dimension" in counseling encourages self-disclosure in psychotherapy and provides more humanistic exchange (Kiesler, 1988). Self-disclosure is contrasted with I:R in Chapter 6.

In contrast to Freud, who severely criticized self-disclosure as a temptation of "young and eager psychoanalysts," stating "the physician should be impenetrable to the patient, and, like a mirror, reflect nothing but what is shown to him" (Goldstein, 1994, p. 417), researchers have shown that self-disclosure facilitates communication and creates positive attributions of counselors (VandeCreek & Angstadt, 1985). Yet risks occur when self-disclosure is used (e.g., individual interest in self-disclosure by participants, when boundaries with participants are unclear, the interviewee feels vulnerable, etc.) (Goldstein, 1994).

In I:R, the process of the interaction and relationship is organized on the basis of the interviewer's adaptation of self-awareness, authenticity, and attunement rather than a specific recommendation that endorses self-disclosure. Unquestionably, the I:R approach finds a parallel in self-disclosure research linking reciprocity—where the disclosure of the counselor (interviewer) stimulates disclosure by the counselee (interviewee), and enhanced therapeutic engagements evolve. I:R, however, does not encourage self-disclosure; it encourages self-awareness, authenticity, and attunement as efforts of the interviewer to participate with the interviewee in a "new space" through a "new relationship" toward understanding.

Moving Beyond Traditional Approaches to Interviewing

Traditionally, the interviewer was equated with an observer. Current research studies have identified the *relationship* as the single most critical aspect present in therapeutic interventions (Luborsky et al., 1986). The *relationship* offers the foundation for healing in therapy; it offers the foundation for a deep and clear comprehension in interviewing. In a review article, Messer (1986) has shown that in recent years, both psychoanalytic and behavioral schools have integrated more personal aspects of the therapist (interviewer), such as the quality of their interaction, dimensions of their relationship, and even personality characteristics and self-revelation. For example, he pointed out, "There have always been psychologists who stressed the therapist's benignity and humaneness," and that more recently, behavioral therapists have reached a consensus "that a positively toned, warm, and caring relationship in an atmosphere of trust may be an important facet of behavior therapy" (p. 1268).

A 1989 review article examined the individual therapist's contribution to the psychotherapeutic process and outcome. The article concluded that although it is difficult to identify the variable explaining the therapist's integral influence on the process of change, "evidence supporting the importance of the individual therapist is widespread" (Lambert, 1989, p. 469).

Yet the relational dimension in interviewing remains an enigma for the field. On one hand, most people agree that a relationship provides the best opportunity for understanding someone; on the other hand, some feel that developing a relationship may confuse the individuals' boundaries. In addition, some feel it is difficult to standardize the interviewing process because each relationship reflects the unique characteristics of the individual. The I:R approach shows how to preserve both the integrity of the boundaries and the relational dimension for the interviewing process.

Various discussions express both the struggles and the progress that interviewers have made concerning this dilemma. For example, David Hutchins proposed guidelines that enable counselors to integrate theory and techniques with each client's behavior to improve the counselor-client relationship (Hutchins, 1984). Clare Brey found that the interviewee's interpretation of the interviewer's nonverbal behavior has a significant impact on the relationship (Brey, 1985). Hans Strupp (1986) worked to distinguish the therapeutic process as a product of "specific" (technique) and "common" (interpersonal) components. He emphasized that psychotherapy is a systematic use of a *human relationship* for therapeutic purposes. Furthermore, Strupp suggested that the therapist creates an "interpersonal context" in addition to attending to formal psychological factors.

Matthews (1988) considers the impact on the encounter of the interviewer's sharing of personal information with the client or patient. His discussion reopens (or opens) the question of the role of personal relationships in the interview process.

In the literature, we find discussions that examine the nature of the therapist's approach to clients in terms of his or her personal development, interpersonal style, and life experiences (Casement, 1991; McCounaughly, 1987; Teyber, 1988). Teyber (1988) emphasizes how the therapist's own personality, developmental history, and current situation are brought into the therapeutic relationship and influence the course of treatment. He insists that human qualities must be used in one's conceptual framework, and that the relationship must hold personal meaning for both participants. Teyber states that "therapists must try to establish a significant emotional relationship with their clients" (p. 13). Such articles underscore the relevance of the interviewer's personal contribution to the quality of an interview. They permit the conclusion that shows increasing support for engaging the interviewer in the interviewing relationship.

The I:R approach emphasizes an actively integrated role for the interviewer in the task and the relationship. This approach assumes that the interviewer can engage in an appropriate relationship within the context of the interview. Toward that interest, I:R requires that the interviewer identify his personal qualities and consider how he may share these in the relationship with the interviewee. As this occurs, the interviewer encourages the interviewee, in turn, to express his or her qualities, thereby deepening the interview. In this way, the interviewer will discover more about the interviewee.

The next chapter shows how the interviewer implements the I:R approach. We will detail specific aspects of how self-awareness and authenticity affect attunement. The chapter answers the basic questions: How can one establish the I:R approach? What can the interviewer do to enhance an interaction and relationship for a successful interview?

3

Creating the Interactive-Relational Interview

By explaining how the interviewer may implement particular actions and draw upon his or her own resourcefulness, this chapter shows how the interviewer shapes an interview and engages the interactive-relational (I:R) approach. Self-awareness, authenticity, and attunement are explored as essential components of the interviewer's repertoire to establish the in-depth interview.

The Interviewer's Role

The interviewer sets the stage for the interviewing process. His or her conduct through the interaction and relationship that is initiated affects the success of the in-depth interview.

The Interviewer's Role
  I. Establishing the Setting
- Identifying goals for oneself
- Explaining goals to the interviewee
- Responding to concerns of the interviewee

  II. Essential Aspects
- Self-awareness (recognition of one's personal beliefs, values, and characteristics)
- Authentic response (tempered by respect and sensitivity)
- Attunement through attending and extending (to establish rapport and to create opportunities to deepen the interview)

  III. Personal Characteristics
- Incorporating one's personal characteristics

Establishing the Setting

The interviewer begins the interviewing process by *identifying* his or her objectives and establishing rapport. By clearly *identifying one's goals* and clarifying one's expectations for an interview, the interview itself is given a course and direction. Additionally, one's professional objectives require reflection. Although the interviewer will establish a relationship, he or she needs to recognize his or her role and professional concern when establishing the tone and course of the I:R interview.

Upon the initial meeting of the interviewee, the interviewer begins to use aspects of the I:R approach (e.g., engagement, attending, and interviewing techniques that instill rapport, such as listening skills and establishing a safe place).

By *explaining the goals* for an interview, the interviewer initiates a collaborative process with the interviewee from the initial engagement.

By *responding to concerns of the interviewee,* the interviewer expresses interest in the interviewee to address factors that may interfere with the process of the interview.

Essential Aspects for Interviewing

The I:R approach draws on the personal qualities of the interviewer. As illustrated in Chapter 1, the particular dimensions that this approach finds essential for success are (a) self-awareness, (b) authenticity, and (c) attunement.

SELF-AWARENESS

Self-awareness entails cognizance, perception, and information concerning one's character, beliefs, traits, and demeanor. The process of self-knowledge is ongoing. Self-awareness facilitates the process of interviewing to the degree that one understands or realizes one's impact on the interviewee. An interviewer's self-awareness allows for the realization that he or she affects and is affected by the interviewee. Knowing details about what one brings to the interview allows one to go beyond the fact-finding part of an interaction toward a direct experience of the nature of the person (which is addressed later in this chapter).

To address aspects of the ways in which self-awareness affects the interviewer:interviewee alliance, authors have linked it to the subject of self-disclosure. The extensive literature on the topic of self-disclosure considers the interrelationship of self-disclosure and personality; the role of self-disclosure on the development, maintenance, and determination of personal relationships; and the contribution of self-disclosure to counseling and psychotherapy (Derlega & Berg, 1987; Nilsson, Strassberg, & Bannon, 1979; VandeCreek & Angstadt, 1985). Research bears evidence that revealing one's situation, thoughts, feelings, or experiences has a positive impact on the therapeutic relationship (Mallinckrodt & Helms, 1986; Peca-Baker & Friedlander, 1989). As the case studies and examples of I:R show, such promising results extend to the interview setting generally. Self-disclosure in I:R, however, is guided by the interviewer's self-awareness, authenticity, and attunement. Self-disclosure results in I:R only in the service of these parameters or ends.

The application of the I:R approach links self-disclosure with reciprocity—where the disclosure of the counselor (interviewer) stimulates disclosure by the counselee (interviewee), and enhanced engagements evolve. In the process of the I:R approach, self-awareness may involve self-disclosure or a conscious participation with the interviewee involving critical and thoughtful consideration of the impact of the disclosure.

In courses that I have taught in both counseling and psychotherapy, I observed that some students were prone to rely on either theoretical approaches and guidelines or the personal engagement that they established. Whereas several students successfully integrated theoretical perspectives with their personal qualities, two other distinct groups emerged: The first group felt self-conscious and inhibited about its role as counselor and worked to incorporate the disciplines of various techniques; the second group quickly engaged in friendly discussions with its role-playing patients. Formalism and awkwardness characterized the interviews of the former group, which attempted to role-play based on applications of formal theories. Carefree and personable qualities characterized the interviews of the latter group, which drew primarily on its own characteristics and intuition. Whereas the former group of students often rigidly applied theory, the latter group of students often lacked critical insight, judgment, and an academic framework. To use the I:R approach successfully, one must integrate knowledge about one's theory, task, and self.

AUTHENTICITY

Authenticity is the genuine, honest, and truthful expression of thoughts, feelings, beliefs, and intents that encourages a reciprocal response by an interviewee. In a safe setting, an interviewer's authenticity invites an open exchange that allays defensiveness.

By acknowledging one's viewpoints, one's honest exchange invites the interviewee to respond in kind, thereby engaging reciprocity. Honest exchange also sets the stage for attunement. In practice, authenticity takes precedence over the imitation of qualities of a theoretical or a professional stance. Therefore, one develops a particular adaptation of I:R on the basis of one's own qualities.

Carl Rogers (1951) advocated using empathy as a required element of interviewing theory. Carl Rogers's effective use of empathy genuinely conveyed his characteristics. Although the usefulness in counseling and interviewing is well-documented, to assume that all persons must, should, or can demonstrate the particular characteristic of empathy effectively to facilitate understanding of another may prove counterproductive to the interview. The I:R approach draws on the interviewer's authentic qualities to advance interviewing.

Healthy boundaries are not violated by the close encounters that evolve as a result of an authentic interaction and relationship. Vignettes in this chapter demonstrate that professional responsibility and clinical judgment need not be forfeited when one uses personal characteristics in the interaction. Moreover, these vignettes detail how the interviewer's authentic expression of personal characteristics provides the opportunity to learn more about an interviewee.

Interviewers (McCracken, 1988; Morrison, 1995) who advocate a formal posture and disregard or minimize authenticity lose the significance and potential for how the interpersonal process facilitates the interview. For example, Grant McCracken (1988), in *The Long Interview,* describes a four-step approach that "gives us the opportunity to step into the mind of another person, to see and experience the world as they do themselves" (p. 9), while advocating that "the interviewer is a benign, accepting, curious (but not inquisitive) individual. . . . It is better to appear slightly dim and too agreeable" (p. 38). "A technique that can be useful for both the interviewer and the respondent is that of 'playing dumb.' . . . They respond with enthusiastic generosity when it appears the interviewer is not very worldly" (p. 40). When interviewers function in such premeditated, manipulative, or "professional" modes, they may achieve certain ends but lose opportunities for deeper engagement and exploration.

Sometimes interviews feign contrived stances. For example, James Morrison (1995) states in *The First Interview,* "If you appear relaxed, interested, and sympathetic, your patient is more likely to feel safe and comfortable" (p. 24). Such stances provide stability through meeting an established expectation, but a contrived demeanor for maintenance of a professional stance may limit the use of other characteristics that an interviewer may possess and incorporate.

ATTUNEMENT

Attunement involves attentiveness to the interviewee as primary. Within the I:R approach, attunement engenders the opportunities for establishing points of contact, the potential for action, and resonation that deepen the interview.

The literature about attunement originated in reference to the relationship of parental styles in child rearing. It explains how when caretakers were attuned to the needs of the child, the child developed a strong sense of self as well as a strong sense of safety to explore his or her environment (Bowlby, 1969; Stern, 1985). Such alert anticipation and care complements both parties

(Kiesler, 1988) and effects reciprocity. In therapy, the importance of effective attunement has achieved value even over the significance of insight (Stolorow, 1991).

As treated in the I:R approach, attunement occurs as a result of the interviewer's attentiveness through the use of verbal and nonverbal actions such as listening skills, eye contact, body language, vocal tone, and speech rate. These actions in I:R operate within the two components of attunement: *attending* and *extending*. Attending requires the interviewer to display care and concern. Extending takes the concern beyond the traditional interview framework in response to the interviewee's needs. Furthermore, attunement resonates with the interviewee, and complementarity deepens the interview: one's motivation pulls motivation, one's friendliness pulls friendliness, one's interest pulls interest. As the mutual attunement occurs, the relational dimension grows. In the face of attentiveness and responsiveness, the interviewee finds safety to explore dimensions of the new relationship, and a deeper awareness of one another emerges, fostering further opportunities to connect and to explore.

On the other hand, a lack of attunement may result because of the lack of cathexis between the interviewer and the interviewee. Some interviewers miss the potential of understanding an interviewee because of their formal, professional focus or their interest in arresting diffuse, unproductive communication. For example, Morrison (1995) directs clinicians "against . . . small talk" (p. 11), arguing that

> in most cases your patient has come for treatment because of troubling problems. Comments about the weather or baseball may seem a distraction, or at worse an expression of unconcern on your part. It is usually better to go right to the heart of the matter. (p. 11)

A highly directed interview may generate data but lose significant information. Morrison's warning about meaningless discussion holds value, but controlled engagement may limit one's opportunity to learn from what occurs between the interviewer and the interviewee.

The depth of an interview correlates with one's growth in self-awareness, authenticity, and attunement to the interviewee. Attunement is not equated with unfocused rumination, and small talk does not equate with attunement. Interviews that are highly directed as well as those that meander lose opportunities for learning about the interviewee.

The Personal Characteristics of
the Interviewer in the I:R Approach

By identifying and incorporating personal characteristics, an interviewer can provide a more authentic interaction. To sensitize interviewers to the significance of using themselves in an interview, interviewers should assess themselves and how they may directly and indirectly affect the interviewing process. One way to obtain self-awareness is to identify personal characteristics. As in the I:R approach, an interviewer's expression of personal characteristics may result in the interviewee's experience or recognition of those characteristics. This may perhaps lead to an appreciation and resonance with the interviewee. This presents the opportunity for mutual attunement and engagement of the potential for action. When integrated, one's personal characteristics are extraordinarily powerful resources for the interviewing process.

In this section, I identify 10 characteristics that I expressed in my interviewing work. Through self-evaluation, each interviewer should identify predominant characteristics that he or she brings to an interview. Although not necessarily used to the same degree in each of the examples that follow, these characteristics were sources for the energizing pulse, resonating with the people interviewed. Such characteristics enhanced the interviewee:interviewer relationship. The degree to which the participants engage and share personal characteristics may dramatically affect the extent to which an interviewer may come to know an interviewee. This being true, each interviewer must assess his or her personal characteristics and recognize how such qualities bear on the interview.

INTEGRITY

Integrity encompasses one's ability to act in an unimpaired, complete, honest manner. We often revisit questions such as "Can I be who I am?" "Am I competent enough?" "Can I say what I really believe?" Such concerns occur around different audiences at different times and, therefore, may require different responses. As I conducted interviews, integrity provided a framework.

For example, my interview with U.S. Supreme Court Justice Sandra Day O'Connor was scheduled to take place in her chambers of the Supreme Court Building in Washington, D.C. As I entered this imposing classical structure, I informed a guard of my appointment. After a security check, he called an

officer to escort me through long corridors toward a room called Lawyer's
Hall. He told me to wait until they called me for my meeting with Justice
O'Connor. I sat in one of two chairs placed in the middle of this ominous room
that was at least three stories high. Although I had walked into the Court
Building feeling cheerful and confident, I now felt my body tense in response
to the formality and security.

After 20 minutes, another guard dutifully entered and accompanied me
to the Justice's Chambers. No discussion transpired as we walked through a
maze of halls. He stoically introduced me to a secretary, who then introduced
me to Justice O'Connor's administrative assistant. Shortly afterwards, Sandra
Day O'Connor came out of her office and greeted me with the firm smile
familiar to me from photographs. She spoke in a measured and deliberate tone
and invited me into her office.

Feeling her controlled behavior before we sat down, I asked if I could
remove my sports jacket, hoping to alleviate the air of formality. She nodded
approvingly. Knowing that she had four sons about my age, I thought that she
might engage in casual conversation. However, she quickly focused on our
interview and, without my prompting, told me that she went to Stanford, her
"first choice," and had not applied to Harvard University. Aware that she knew
of my Harvard affiliation, I found her statement provocative.

Because she started speaking immediately, I asked her if she could wait
a moment until I could start the tape recorder. To my astonishment, she
informed me that she did not permit recording of her interviews. Her remark
caught me off guard, and I stopped. Furthermore, she instructed me to put the
recorder away. Anticipating my "appeal," she told me that I should have "no
problem" in transcribing our interview, remarking that she transcribed all the
discussion that took place during closed sessions of the Supreme Court, where
tape recording was prohibited. Hardly taking a breath, she made it clear that
she transcribed because she was, at that time, the most junior member of the
Court, not because she was a woman. Moments into the interview, I felt
bombarded by negative elements and up against a dilemma.

I persisted regarding my need to record because I thought that having to
take notes would greatly interfere with the interviewing process. She argued
that it would not and reaffirmed her decision that I "could not" record our
discussion as she firmly placed both hands over her lap. We were at a
stalemate. I realized that she would not change her mind. I felt this interview
stood on the precipice of conclusion. In an effort to respect both of our
concerns, I suggested that we treat our meeting as a *consultation* about the

subject of the interview that might serve as a preface for my book. I thought this might get us over the hurdle. She agreed, I did not tape-record, and finally our discussion began.

Although we had arranged for a 1-hour interview, we spoke for more than 2 hours. Although the meeting was informative, I did not feel that I had engaged her as I had hoped. Transcribing notes might prove an adequate way for the Supreme Court to articulate their findings, but I did not believe that it would capture the character and the life of Justice O'Connor.

We discussed a great deal of material and departed on more than cordial terms. Before leaving, she called her assistant and asked her to give me a personal tour of the Supreme Court. After exchanging good-byes with Justice O'Connor, her assistant congratulated me on what she found an unusual situation—Justice O'Connor had exceeded the allotted 1 hour. Although disappointed because I could not record the interview, I was assured by her assistant that the Justice must have been interested in our discussion because she was normally rigorous about her schedule. She even extended an invitation for a tour of the building.

I reconstructed my interview with Justice O'Connor and sent her a transcript, including a note of appreciation for her time. I reiterated that I would treat our meeting as a consultation and expressed a desire to meet again. Shortly afterwards, she sent me a letter indicating that we could meet again to pursue the project. This time she allowed the recording.

This vignette highlights the importance of attunement to the interviewee and maintaining integrity with respect to our work. In my request to remove my sports coat, I attempted to bring a level of comfort to myself, to Justice O'Connor, and to an austere setting. I knew that a mere reconstruction of conversation from transcribed notes would not reveal the experience. As I expressed my thoughts, feelings, and needs about the recording directly, I attended to her needs by adjusting my goal for our interview. I did not select a combative, firm position in response to her decision that we not record the first interview. Had I pretended to feel satisfied with her request not to tape, we would not have encountered each other as people with particular preferences and agendas. In addition, we would not have had the opportunity to explore how we could manage a difference of opinion. This gave me greater insight into her personal style; it gave us insight into one another. In selecting a middle ground appropriate to the project, I attended to and respected her needs. Therefore, we both maintained integrity. In this way, Justice O'Connor came to know me personally, even though I had not felt that we initially engaged as I had intended, to understand the project, and eventually to feel comfortable enough to participate in the project willingly, allowing subsequent taping to take place.

The inherent risk, as in any interview, is that she would not have shared with me her story. Quite possibly, an interviewer using traditional methods might acquiesce to her request or firmly disagree. A prescribed format would not permit the interviewer to act according to his or her beliefs or feelings about this stalemate.

Her wish to prohibit the recording did not necessarily demonstrate obstinance. Although I pursued her reluctance, she responded vaguely without definitive reason. Regardless of her reasons, this encounter permitted Justice O'Connor to observe and experience my integrity related to my work and for me to respect the integrity of her wishes. This provided an opportunity to unveil a shared characteristic, integrity, related to our approach to work.

MOTIVATION

Motivation is a personal incentive and interest. As a characteristic, it advances one's goal; as a shared experience, it sustains an interview. Jeane Kirkpatrick stands out as a respected, serious, academic figure. I felt we could engage each other at the academic level, and I respected her leadership. However, the media's characterizations about Dr. Kirkpatrick's personality concerned me.

Characterizations of Jeane Kirkpatrick included the "iron woman," "cold," "a boxer of the mind," and "hypercritical"—in fact, words that engendered her first moments with me. She challenged the rationale of my study on women, asking for "definitions." I answered her questions and returned the challenges. We both seemed to appreciate the intellectual stimulation. We visibly enjoyed each other's checks, as evidenced from her supportive comments to her cajoling grin, and continued beyond these intellectual challenges to specific topics of concern. As we discussed her personal life, I learned that Jeane Kirkpatrick had been misunderstood. She was bright and confrontational, yet playful. By her account, her true love lay not in defeating men or in winning arguments but in enjoying her womanhood, being a mother, a lover. She described these roles with the utmost conviction, emotion, and excitement. As she reflected on her role as mother, I felt the profound meaning that this experience held for her:

Nothing in life can compare. To give birth is a wonderful experience! It is by far the best part of being a woman. It is *remarkable; fantastic;* no words are adequate to say it. I only wish that I could maximize those moments of being a mother, to *exploit* the very seconds of those moments of sharing life with my sons. It is so sensual, and it is the very essence of life.

The more I spoke with her, the more absorbed I became in our discussion. I enjoyed being with her and listening to her talk about those things most important in her life. Two things about her became dominant motivating factors that made me want to pursue our relationship: She expressed a passion for life, and she could identify clearly her values and what held significance for her. We were mutually motivated in discussing the philosophy of life. We met several times over a few years.

In this example, we observe that personal characteristics can resonate and engage in-depth communication. Even when participants share characteristics, however, resonation may not occur between the participants to culminate in a rich inner view. I cite my experience with Billie Jean King.

Her athletic achievements attracted me to understand this female athlete. We met in her office in New York City. She seemed unassuming and conversant. Yet her remarks seemed perfunctory and rehearsed. We discussed her career and eventually talked about her lesbian orientation. Her nonverbal cues reflected her discomfort in discussing the latter issue.

To confirm this, she stated that she did not want to discuss an issue that had become fodder for newspapers. In addition, she seemed more interested in responding to the frequent interruptions that disturbed our interview. The combination of these interruptions and the lack of her investment in our conversation trivialized the issues and precluded our opportunity to connect.

In the end, I found that we could not engage the potential for action because of the lack of motivation. Although we individually shared the characteristic of motivation in our respective fields, and I was motivated to know her, the motivation did not resonate between us because Billie Jean King did not have a desire to engage fully in the interview. Although sharing personal characteristics is very helpful to engage the potential for action, it does not alone account for the successful interview.

In my interview with Billie Jean King, her motivation was not directed toward engaging and deepening the interview. In my interview with Jeane Kirkpatrick, her motivation emerged forcefully. My appreciation and identification of her motivation resonated with my own. As we proceeded, this deepened our exchange.

Although both individuals may possess the same quality, the interview may be limited unless there is reciprocal attunement. Reciprocal interest to continue engaging is required in the development of the I:R approach.

TRUST

The best way to recognize trust, reliance, belief, or faith in another is to experience it. Psychologists inform us that the ability to trust emerges out of our first experiences with significant others who love us and with whom we feel confident (Erikson, 1964; Kilpatrick, 1975). The lack of such encounters leaves indelible scars that block the development of this trait. We intuitively thirst for love; if we are deprived of this drink, trusting becomes difficult.

As in the story of the prisoner Randy, my actions on his behalf provided him with evidence that I trusted him. In this case, taking risks with colleagues, with a superior's judgment, and even with personal safety created a trusting situation that increased Randy's esteem and trust for me and strengthened our relationship. Randy was keenly sensitive to my actions and responded by trusting me through sharing his deep, innermost feelings revealed in his poems and, subsequently, through direct dialogue. These gestures impelled freedom and openness, establishing opportunities for the potential for action.

OPENNESS

Openness suggests accessibility, vulnerability, and a lack of pretense. Donna Summer told me that she almost cancelled our interview because she dreamed I was an old, bearded, Harvard professor with a pipe who would interrogate her. When I learned of her anxieties, I shared with her my own concerns. I told Ms. Summer that at the beginning of this project, I was self-conscious. "How would the renowned women in this study perceive me? . . . What could I say to them?"

Such appropriate disclosures aided my interviewees and helped us to overcome our fears and private anxieties and discard the masks created by our roles. Our initial images of one another did not dictate the course of our interaction. As interviewer, I helped shift our preinterview impressions. Impressions often emanate from hearsay determined by the subjective judgments of others. Being open to an experience and about one's own thinking provides the opportunity for participating in new awareness.

EMPATHY

Empathy enhances an interview. It embodies understanding so intimate that feelings, thoughts, and motives of one are readily comprehended by another. In I:R, empathy moves in two directions: from the interviewer to the interviewee and from the interviewee to the interviewer. This reciprocation of empathy may cause role confusion if the interviewer loses sight of the goal of the interview. However, role confusion does not necessarily result from reciprocation. Therefore, concern of role confusion need not limit or inhibit the interviewer's empathy or deprive it from meeting its potential.

A deeper encounter often results when the interviewee and interviewer can empathize with each other. When I read over the transcripts of my interviews, I recognized reciprocal empathy in most of them. Role confusion did not take place.

I offer the following two examples in which I have encountered such reciprocated empathy.

Bette Davis

My interviews with Bette Davis ran a gamut of comportment from her first theatrical greeting in the hallway of her home, when she literally dressed for the occasion, to discussions over hard drinks when she felt no compulsion to wear makeup. Over the period of our work, her language shifted from rehearsed script to self-revealing responses and to inquiries directed about me:

> *When* do I get to find out about *you?* . . . I would love to do what you're doing, to *study* people, to *talk* with them about what *really* matters. . . . You've asked about my life. My life is playing the *roles* of real life and real people. You're a *real* person. You're with people in the action of their life. I'm sure that your life is more interesting than mine. During the time that we've spoken, I have often thought about you, your day, the fact that you are one of those *real* people.

The quality of the engagement attests to shared empathy reinforced through the I:R components of shared attending, extending, and reciprocity. Bette Davis verbalized the experience of the I:R approach. Her attunement demonstrated incisive identification, not only showing how she observed my role but how she understood my activities: "You're with people in the action of their life."

B. F. Skinner

B. F. Skinner did not characteristically express feelings directly. Dr. Skinner generally managed his feelings through actions. On one occasion, Skinner recommended that I review a book that he thought would help me with a paper that I was writing. He had said that he would bring the book with him to our next meeting. When we had lunch at a local restaurant, he realized that he had forgotten it. He apologized and wanted to return to his office to get it. Although I felt that this could wait, he insisted we go back. He instructed me to stay in my car. Despite being ill and in his mid 80s, he insisted on climbing the seven flights of stairs (because the elevators were inoperative) of William James Hall at Harvard to get the book. After he returned, I observed his pleasure in being able to do something for me.

When the interviewee is empathic, one should not automatically equate such expressions as niceties or examine such actions only in terms of a hidden agenda. One should experience such empathy as an opportunity to develop the relationship more deeply. The urge to give and take naturally emerges from relationships. Such empathic demonstrations show the reciprocity occurring in the relationship of the I:R approach.

INSIGHT

Insight involves the capacity to elucidate the true nature of a situation; it reflects a penetrating grasp of the matter at hand. Insight is one's recognition of what one intuitively understands.

For example, a lawyer referred a teenager to me for a consultation. The 15-year-old boy had been charged with three counts of assault and battery and 10 counts of breaking and entering. Looking at least 20 years old, the teenager, whom I will call Danny, was tall, large-framed, and aggressive. I asked him to tell me about himself. He said that he was Italian and paused, as if that explained his identity. He communicated in telegraphic, short, unemotional responses. He prided himself in telling me that he was a "block leader." He claimed that the police would not have caught him except that his friend had not as skillfully covered his tracks. In the course of our interview, Danny shared that his greatest enjoyment was in beating up older men and stealing cars to rip out their radios. He took pride in his machismo manner as he described his strategies for car theft. His eyes glistened, and he became energized and animated. Although he did not present himself as intelligent, I was struck by the acumen he demonstrated in his descriptions of the planning and execution of his crimes.

Based on my growing awareness of his intelligence (insight), I decided to recommend that we conduct a full psychological battery. Danny had an IQ of 130+ (intellectually superior) on the verbal subtests (that indicate one's thinking potential) and 95 (meaning borderline normal) on performance subtests (that indicate one's actual functioning). He was clinically depressed, and his performance fell far below his abilities. Through this assessment process, Danny appeared intrigued by the positive information that he learned about himself. In one test, a person repeats a series of up to nine numbers stated by the examiner. By choice, Danny repeated the numbers not only in accurate order but also in reverse order. In our sessions, he began smiling, laughing, and telling me stories about his life. His increased self-awareness ignited insightfulness both cognitively and personally. He had begun to feel success.

Danny experienced increased confidence resulting from my insight that we explore his abilities through this encounter. He became motivated, developing intellectual curiosity and a desire to deepen his participation in the interviewing process.

NURTURANCE

Holistically, our biological, psychological, and spiritual systems require appropriate nurturance for good health. Nurturance is the act of sustaining and enhancing development and growth. Without it, these systems become unbalanced and often contorted in their effort to survive. Nurturance demands more than unconditional support; it demands giving of one's self personally.

One young woman named Mary, whom I had treated for an anxiety disorder, asked me to see her boyfriend. Her boyfriend, Jim, was using cocaine and abusing alcohol. Mary's growth in counseling led her to make more healthy decisions about her life. She felt that unless Jim stopped the substance abuse, she would have to end the relationship. To ease Jim into treatment, she told him that his appointment with me was to help him deal with her. She felt that if he gave himself a chance, he would respond to the counseling experience.

Jim was in his early 20s. He had quit college and worked in a blue-collar job. He was the middle child of a large Irish-Catholic family. His father had died when he was 4 years old, and, in the face of adversity, he had learned to keep a "stiff upper lip," not to express his feelings, and to act tough. Jim was forceful and masculine. I also found him very sensitive and bright.

Our initial contact permitted a careful review of his life as he expressed ease in our first meeting. He responded very positively to care and support. He told me that he had not shared with anyone the personal matters that he brought to our session. A symbol of felt nurturance was expressed on one occasion when he brought a full-course meal to the therapy session that he wanted to share with me. Upon further inquiry, I learned that it was his experience of identifying with me and feeling nurturance that freed him to share the struggles in his life.

TRUTH

Truth implies fidelity to an original standard based in reality. The search for truth is the basic drive in my life. The pursuit of truth enabled me to persevere beyond B. F. Skinner's image as an atheist and even self-attributed agnostic to one who struggled with spiritual matters. Chapter 4 reviews several interviews that I conducted with him over a 20-year period. The process of these interviews documents how my search for truth resulted in a unique and genuine understanding of the man.

The mutual appreciation of the search for truth explains to a great degree why Skinner agreed to meet with me weekly over the past 5 years of his life to discuss carefully questions of psychology, philosophy, and religion. Because we both sought truth, we gave each other sustenance. This truth resonated between us and bonded our relationship.

RESPECT

Respecting, considering, and honoring an interviewee's wishes and privacy has played an essential role for everyone I have interviewed. One can convey respect through confidentiality. Professional settings demand it; good journalism ensures it. Moreover, respect involves attunement, attending to and valuing the person who entrusts him- or herself to you.

If a relationship develops, the interviewer awakens heightened sensitivities in the interviewee and must protect his or her needs, vulnerabilities, and secrets. This conveys the respect the interviewer has for the interviewee and serves as the litmus test in a relationship. To fail this test usually causes all of the work, regardless of how involved and well-intended, to crumble.

After knowing Donna Summer for several years, I recall her saying to me at her home, "You never ask me for anything." She explained, "I've waited to see if you would, and here it is five years, and you still have not asked me to do something for you. . . . By now they usually do." In interviews, the interviewer must act with clarity and caution while maintaining professional boundaries.

FAITH

Faith, one's beliefs, and the ways in which one construes meaning affect one's experience and perception of the world. Gordon Allport (1968) characterized the assumptions of the nature of the "person" for the major schools of psychological thought and explained how one's philosophical perception results in a psychological analysis consistent with that interpretation. For example, in the Skinnerian view, the person is seen as a "reactive being" because the counselor is likely to think of his or her client in terms of past conditioning and potential reconditioning or in terms of reinforcements and environmental determinism. In the Freudian view, the human is understood as "reactive being in-depth" because the counselor is likely to think of the client in terms of the unconscious processes and causation. In the Rogerian view, the person is seen as "being in process"—one who is evolving toward a more or less directed goal. Similarly, I think that each person's perception about human nature comes into play in an interview.

I bring more than assumptions about people to an interview. I identify this as my "faith," a system of spiritual principles and beliefs. In Greek, the noun "faith" (*pistis*) is also a verb (*pistevo*) expressing action: an active "believing process" about the sacred dimension of human beings. Such faith is operative in my interview process.

My faith holds that all human beings possess intrinsic gifts, including rational faculties; moral sensibilities; intuition; creativity; free will; the ability to rise above impulses; and to love God, self, and others. I approach people with an interest to discover their individual expression of these dimensions. The seeds of these faculties can develop in each person and lead each toward a wider awareness of self, others, and life. These "gifts" complement each other, allow for mutual growth, and unite people.

The I:R approach both originates and results from understandings about broadening one's self-awareness. Through identifying one's personal characteristics, the interviewer becomes aware of resources within him- or herself that may enhance communication and highlight the importance for clarifying which qualities the interviewee possesses. The self-evaluation in Appendix A may help you to identify qualities that you may use in your adaptation of the I:R approach.

Having completed the inventory in Appendix A, select your 10 most prominent characteristics. Do you feel that you convey these qualities when you conduct an interview? How might your characteristics affect your interviews?

Identification of one's characteristics provides a step toward becoming self-aware. It may be helpful to ask a close friend to evaluate you on the same scale to expand your awareness. This inventory should help you begin the process of awareness as you conduct the I:R approach.

In addition, one needs to monitor the impact of less desirable, perhaps even negative characteristics on an interviewee. At times, even characteristics that we consider positive and use accordingly may have an unproductive effect on the interview.

Throughout this chapter, we have identified the importance of the interviewer's role: establishing the setting; the essential aspects of self-awareness, authenticity, and attunement; and identification and integration of the interviewer's characteristics. In relation to the aforementioned aspects, the interviewer in I:R should also recognize the impact of his or her beliefs and values.

Beliefs and Values

In an effort to know someone, acknowledgment of one's own beliefs and values and recognition of those of another may very appropriately surface in an interview. This does not require that one should express one's beliefs or values, but it suggests the awareness of the often powerful significance of such concerns for the individual as well as how beliefs and values may affect an interview.

Harvard Medical School professor Thomas Gutheil reports the reaction of medical school residents, whom he instructs on how to conduct a patient history. These psychiatric residents, without batting an eye, obtain a complete sexual history, including positions, lubricants, erotic devices, and the like. In response to his counsel that a medical history include information about a patient's religion, Dr. Gutheil recalls the common reaction of residents, who say, "Isn't that too personal?" or "That's very private information!" He quipped, "Following a detailed sexual history they react about the propriety of asking about one's religious beliefs!"

An interviewer, however, should discern the necessity of disclosing one's own beliefs and values as well as pursue discussion about such matters with an interviewee (see discussions in Chapters 1 and 2 about self-disclosure, as well as Chapter 6).

I recall interviewing a woman for an administrative assistant position. Her presentation and credentials appeared impeccable. Following careful scrutinizing and several interviews, she was hired. Once on the job, however, she informed me that she would not be able to stay. When I inquired, I learned that she was a member of the Jehovah's Witness faith and, from her religious perspective, she could not be employed in a position that included preparing a newsletter to Christian interdisciplinary professionals. Had the interview explored this facet or the candidate's beliefs and values, this problem could have been avoided.

Likewise, in therapy, when one's values conflict with the behavior or orientation of patients on moral grounds, the interviewer needs to respond genuinely. For example, in a situation where a patient is planning an abortion, and an interviewer holds religious beliefs in opposition to abortion, the interviewer has a responsibility to own his or her predicament and either refer the patient to another clinician or permit the patient to make an informed decision to pursue counseling conscious of the clinician's perspective.

In the I:R approach, an interviewer should recognize the role of beliefs and values out of ethical considerations that can enable the participants to avoid potential roadblocks, clear uncertainties, and conduct open and honest communication. Through awareness and responsiveness to the interviewee's most central nature and concerns, the interviewer expresses ability to engage the interviewee at the deepest and most profound level.

Stages of the I:R Interview

Chapter 1 introduced the concept of the I:R approach, and Chapter 3 addressed the role of interviewee and explained how the interviewer shapes the interviewing process.

Figure 3.1 delineates the progression of the I:R approach in four stages.

56

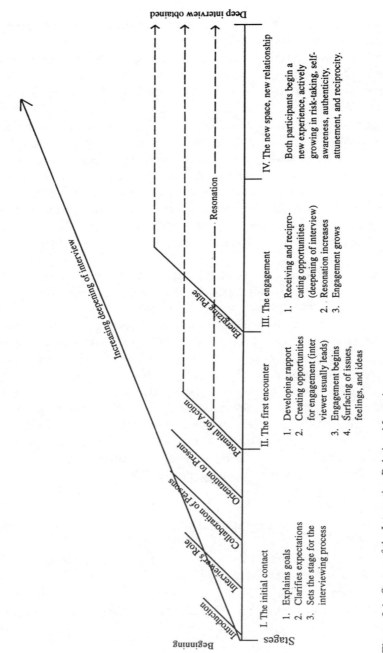

Figure 3.1. Stages of the Interactive-Relational Interview

Stage 1 involves the initial contact. Here, the interviewer introduces his or her purpose and explains the goals, collaboratively clarifying expectations and setting the stage. The interviewer engages I:R, incorporating the I:R way of thinking or understanding of people. The interviewer draws on his or her own qualities, confirms a course, and initiates a present orientation with the interviewee.

Stage 2, the first encounter, marks the initiation of the interview. At this point, rapport is sought. The interviewer attempts to create opportunities to engage the interviewee such that he or she participates in the experience of the interview through sharing him- or herself, responding and engaging the potential for action.

Stage 3, the engagement, shows how increased interaction evolves as the participants raise opportunities to connect through reciprocation. The energizing pulse confirms the realization of the potential for action in the form of resonation and reciprocation.

Stage 4, the new space—the new relationship, marks the participants' entrance into the new space where their relationship reflects refined and frequent reciprocity through risk-taking or attunement and expansion of the relationship. The in-depth interview is obtained.

When most people begin interviewing, they tend not to account fully for the significance of their posture, an approach expressed verbally and nonverbally that conveys their attitude and establishes the terms of the relationship with the interviewee. In Chapter 4, we will present several models that demonstrate the impact of posturing illustrated by the author's experiences with B. F. Skinner.

4

Posturing in the Interview

Interviews are interactional events (Holstein & Gubrium, 1995). In the inter-active-relational (I:R) approach, we observe that the interaction of the interviewer is basically formed through the posture that he or she establishes. The interviewer may find it helpful to identify the posture in his or her approach through assessing his or her participation in the action of an interview.

Models for Interviewing

The following models illustrate various ways in which an interviewer may establish the posture, interaction, and exchange of an interview. Although the succession of the models does not reflect an evolution of one's interviewing technique, these models illustrate that an interviewer's particular interactions with an interviewee affect the outcome of an interview. These models result from a variety of factors, including one's individual experience, character, and perceptions, as well as training about interviewing.[1]

Legend:
E = Interviewee   • = Issue
R = Interviewer   O = Sphere of influence

THE MONOLITHIC MODEL

The **monolithic model** inhibits the active presence of the interviewer. In this model, the interviewer assumes a passive posture while observing and listening to the interviewee. This situation results from either a passive interviewer or an interviewee who assumes control. In either case, inequality emerges. The passive role of the interviewer distorts reality, suggesting only one person's presence. This model isolates the interviewee and negates the impact of any interactions with the interviewer. Because this approach renders a monologue by the interviewee, we often end up with a well-rehearsed script, a data sampling, and an interview that does not reflect engagement, challenge, and fresh thought. The limited interaction results in a limited understanding of the person.

THE MONOLITHIC MODEL REVERSED

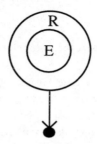

The **monolithic model reversed** shows how the interviewer can dominate an interview. In this model, the interviewer's posturing subjugates the interviewee, addressing the concerns of the interviewer. Because the interviewee cannot carve out his or her role, no dialogue or communication occurs.

This posturing leaves one unable to alter preconceived notions or perceptions of the interviewee.

THE BECLOUDED MODEL

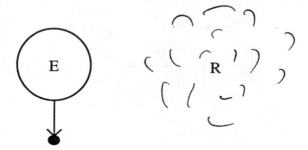

The **beclouded model** acknowledges the interviewer's presence. How-ever, little, if any, interaction occurs. The interviewer and interviewee assume highly formalized roles limiting the interaction and negating the relationship. As a result, the interviewer fails to engage the interviewee. This model may relegate the interviewee to the role of subject and the interviewer to the role of observer. The relationship of interviewer and interviewee becomes objec-tive and distant but not substantive or penetrating.

THE POLARIZED MODEL

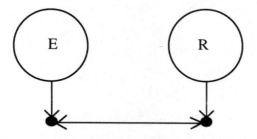

The **polarized model** acknowledges the different perspectives that the interviewer and interviewee may have about particular issues. However, the posturing results in focusing on those issues without regard to the interaction or relationship of the participants. Each speaks from his or her own point of view. The interviewer expresses a perspective, and the interviewee offers an antithetical position, and vice versa. Such posturing highlights unidirectional, fixed, and uncompromising perspectives on issues that often lead to characterizing an individual solely on the basis of his or her stand. This model allows limited interaction without relational exchange.

THE CORRECTIVE MODEL

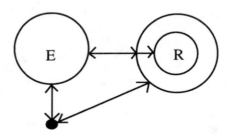

In the **corrective model,** the interviewer recasts the interviewee's perspective on the basis of the interviewer's own conscious or unconscious expectations. The corrective model has a primary commitment to the interests of the interviewer. Therefore, the interviewer's posturing relegates the interviewee's role to a secondary position. This model asserts the knowledge, interests, and authority of the interviewer over the perspective of the interviewee.

THE DIALOGICAL MODEL

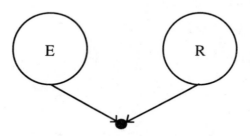

In the **dialogical model,** the interviewer and interviewee engage in conversation about a particular topic from their own perspectives. While valuing the thoughts of each other, it allows the participants to share various points of view and may permit revision. It does not, however, provide a way to involve the individuals on a personal level. This model makes available the information sought and offers the opportunity to revise one's methods, commitments, or thoughts.

THE THEORETICAL MODEL

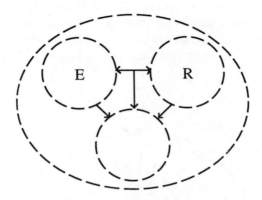

The **theoretical model** describes and promises productive, fulfilling, and revelatory interaction through communication between the participants. However, this model does not realize its potential. The interviewer and the interviewee intend to engage in an "open discussion" or "free dialogue," but they do not put into practice the theory or intent. The dotted lines of the diagram emphasize the theoretical nature of this approach over a concrete process in the interview. The model fails to unite the participants and remains only an ideal. In this approach, people may feel positive about their intentions or about the interview, but the goals remain elusive.

THE DYNAMIC MODEL

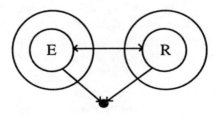

The **dynamic model** identifies the boundaries and methods for interactive communication between the interviewer and the interviewee. It separates the topic or issue that the two discuss from the communication that takes place between them. With this posturing, the interviewer and interviewee can engage in conversation about a particular topic from their own, as well as each other's, perspectives. This model provides the opportunity for change and growth between them. It may act as a precursor to the I:R approach. However, this model does not fully incorporate the roles played by the interviewer and interviewee—their individual characteristics, their personalities, and their histories.

THE I:R MODEL

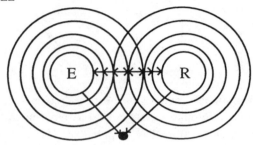

   The **I:R model** incorporates the purposes of the dynamic model and emphasizes the importance of the growing interaction and relationship between interviewer and interviewee. Such posturing illustrates *how* a person communicates on a given topic and, furthermore, requires that both participants explore, wonder, and reflect on their thoughts together. The model best achieves its intentions through the mutual sharing of both parties. Although this interview may begin with a particular topic of discussion, it evolves into an interaction where an exchange of thoughts, beliefs, and emotions takes place, "the new space." The interviewer and the interviewee develop a relationship in which they may gain deeper awareness of each other and themselves. This model draws on the participants who serve as resources for identification, revelation, and understanding, and thereby as the means for deepening the relationship.

B. F. Skinner: Applications of Models

   In this section, I present three different models of interviews that I experienced with an interviewee. Each model reflects a different posture. This presentation shows how these different postures result in different understandings about an interviewee—in this case, B. F. Skinner.

As a social and behavioral science major in college, I was especially interested in understanding the nature of human beings. Philosophical and religious perspectives were equally significant for my intellectual pursuits. At the time, experimental and behavioral psychology dominated the field. I asked myself, Does behavioral psychology adequately explain the nature of a person? I wondered, Does behaviorism alone define human beings? In part, behaviorism seemed to dovetail with my religious beliefs. Jesus said, "Not what goes into the mouth defiles a man but what comes out" (Matthew 15:11). Thus, one's behavior is what counts. Does this sufficiently explain the person?

MONOLITHIC INTERVIEWING

B. F. Skinner was preeminent in the field of behaviorism. As the architect of operant conditioning and the father of behaviorism, he espoused the philosophy that environmental contingencies shape behavior. His studies explained how operant conditioning enabled autistic children to learn and how therapy based on behavioral analysis and behavior modification significantly helped people suffering from a range of problems, from drug addiction to phobias.

However, Skinner based the science of behaviorism upon determinism: a view of human beings as programmed, predetermined, and without free will. This perspective negated religion and God. Was Skinner correct? Although his research yielded significant results, when I read it I felt a profound dichotomy between Skinner's findings and my belief.

I learned that Skinner would be speaking at the Morse Auditorium at Boston University and opted to attend. Seating some 700, the auditorium filled beyond capacity. As he approached the stage, religious protest groups picketed on one side, and Skinner devotees vigorously applauded on the other. Even though I could not quite articulate or explain my dissatisfaction with his lecture, I felt that his perspective did not fairly consider the range of human experience.

That week, I wrote him a brief note expressing my belief that his approach, which emphasized the "form" behaviors take in life, did not address the "content" of life experiences. Because I did not feel that his presentation answered my questions, I requested more information. To my surprise, Dr. Skinner sent me a note recommending that we meet.

I was delighted to have the opportunity to ask questions about the meaning of life to someone whose philosophy of life dramatically differed from mine. This meeting symbolized a confrontation in which I envisioned how "the truth" that I read in psychology compared with "the truth" in faith that I had adopted for my life. I anticipated that he might affirm or challenge my direction, and that this interaction could reveal answers to my personal struggles. Were the allegiances that I had in life concerning truth and faith compatible, different, better, or worse than those of this leading psychologist?

As I entered his secretary's office, I could see Dr. Skinner seated. He stood up as I walked into the room with his assistant. After greeting me rather formally, he invited me to sit and inquired about my thoughts. I immediately set up my recorder and referred to my notes for questions.

Segments of that interview follow. Note that Dennis Tedlock's proposal for translation (see Chapter 2) calls for changing the line in transcription at pauses taken by the participants. Over the three interviews with B. F. Skinner, one observes the increased frequency of pauses, reflecting additional re-examination and thoughtfulness, progressing from the monolithic model to the polarized model to the I:R model.

BFS = B. F. Skinner
JC = John T. Chirban
Date: November, 1972

(Reading from my notes, I inquired:)

JC: If man does not have a choice, does it matter what you are or I am doing? What would be, would be.

BFS: Well, what are you reading?

(His question surprised me. I had come seeking answers, and I immediately inferred that he asked his question to make the point of his own position. Rather than responding directly to my questions, he drew me into his mode of thought.)

JC: Well, it depends upon your values.

(I approached our interview from a faith-based perspective whereas he approached it from a behavioral point of view. This made it virtually impossible to develop a collaborative focus in our interaction.)

BFS: You mean that you would not make a decision to read? Do you understand what I am getting at?

> You see these as self-generated understandings of conduct, presented by
>   contingencies.
> Cultures set up these contingencies of reinforcement. In such situations,
>   you follow the rules of being shaped by the consequences . . .

(His responses to my questions focused on his perspective and lacked
attention to my concern from my perspective. I could not understand his
position yet felt drawn into his thinking. We communicated using different
vocabularies. I felt unprepared for a technical discussion and dialogue. Because
of this dynamic and my posturing, Skinner was dominating the discussion.)

JC: So you don't see a choice?

BFS: No, not at all. . . . You drive a car according to the results and
reinforcements which your movements make. There is no choice.

JC: I'm having difficulty understanding this.

BFS: No, there are just influences on you. . . .
Our behaviors are contingency shaped.

(Skinner's responses were technical, based on concrete, action-oriented
metaphors. Overwhelmed by the certainty of his answers, I felt confronted
by my inability to articulate and his inability or unwillingness to address
my discomfort.)

JC: But isn't it logical that you can decide which reinforcements you will
follow?

BFS: Well . . .
yes. . . .
You can follow your own advice, but that does not control what will
happen. . . .
Of course, you can have a fatalistic philosophy.

(As he addressed the subject of external contingencies in response to my
questions, Skinner negated my interest to address an "inner volition.")

JC: But does that mean if we know enough of the variables, we could
understand, for example, what B. F. Skinner will do?

BFS: Well, it depends on what the culture teaches.

(At this point, Skinner elaborated on details of his theory [deleted from
this transcript].)

JC: But don't you make a distinction between the mechanical aspects, or the
            forms, and the *content,* or the *experience?*

(He wanted to pursue his agenda without attending to my difficulties
about what he proposed. In addition, he continued to dominate the interview
by deflecting my questions.)

BFS: I don't know what you're talking about. What is "content?"

JC: I believe that it is the experience of life's meaning,
            feelings, or purpose.

BFS: I don't know what you mean by feelings.
            Discussion about feelings,
            especially as presented by Freud,
            have gotten us into a lot of trouble,
            wasted a lot of time.

JC: But I think "the fruits of inner life"—prayer and personal
            development—have given such richness to the world.

BFS: Well, I'll take the fruit,
            but I do not know what "content" means,
            if meaning is to be taken seriously.

The course of our discussion was frustrating. On one hand, I was a novice
in the language of behavioral analysis, and Skinner did not follow in the
language of faith. At many times when I attempted, Skinner seemed to ignore
my effort to reach him. It seemed that we used two different languages and
espoused two different epistemologies. This interview lacked engagement.
On the other hand, I wanted to press for answers to some of my personal
dilemmas about life and truth. However, I retreated from challenging him and
became passive when I found him maintaining a fixed perspective.

In this interview, I assumed passive posturing, whereas he seized control. As
the interviewer in the monolithic model, I observed and listened to Dr. Skinner
without an ability to assert control and establish rapport and reciprocity.

POLARIZED INTERVIEWING

Convinced that the spiritual life held empirical validation, I decided to
study the integration of religion and science in my graduate work at Harvard.
Although it had been several years since I had last spoken with Dr. Skinner,
I knew that he regarded the concept of motivation as unnecessary. Neverthe-

less, I felt that his critique of motivation could strengthen my dissertation, so I requested a meeting.

Dr. Skinner agreed to serve as a consultant for my dissertation. We met five times to exchange views on the concepts. These meetings allowed me to reopen some of the same questions we had identified in our initial meeting several years previously.

In the discussions, Skinner explained how past reinforcements and contingencies in the present environment determine behaviors. Thus, "there is no need to bother with will, thoughts, constructs, or motivation."

Skinner argued against "the impractical use of inner causes." Such causes, he said, are either deduced from an independent empirical variable or from a dependent behavior variable, and "so long as the inner event is inferred, it is in no sense an explanation of the behavior and adds nothing to a functional analysis." Although Dr. Skinner graciously participated in the study, his position remained unchanged. Because I could now readily communicate in the terminology of behavioral analysis, I thought we might engage in a dialogue about my concerns with his work.

This time, I prepared myself for the meeting with studies and citations from research. For example, I referenced Rose and Woolsey (McV. Hunt, 1965), who identified portions of the cerebrum related to intrinsic activity, and Olds and Olds (1965), whose contributions on drives and "creative" behavior, even in rats, demonstrated that one could scientifically document motivation that substantiated my position (Chirban, 1981; McV. Hunt, 1965). In this way, I hoped that Skinner could hear my perspective. Skinner replied:

Date: January, 1977

BFS: But I don't like to use the word motivation.
             We are talking about extrinsic and intrinsic reinforcers.
             When you do something, it is because of either internal or external
                consequences. Internal consequences can be something like
                self-stimulation—
             say, scratching an itch. Nobody contrives it; it doesn't require any other
                part of the world.
             There are more subtle examples:
             I push something and it moves. The moving reinforces my push.
             The human species is apparently reinforced when its behavior produces
                effects quite apart from specific effects.
             If I push and it doesn't move, behavior is extinguished.

Or, to take another example, if I put on the wrong glasses, things are
    distorted, and I cannot reach effectively and touch an object.
As to extrinsic reinforcers, I pick an apple and eat it.
The consequence, the flavor of the apple,
is extrinsic. It can be used as a reinforcer.
Someone can give you an apple
to get a favor. Extrinsic reinforcers are outside the skin and require
    external mediation of some kind. Verbal behavior is reinforced both
    extrinsically and intrinsically—
extrinsically by listeners,
intrinsically by the speaker. If you like poetry,
you can recite poetry yourself.

(Skinner sounded as though he recited a well-rehearsed script. The question
from my perspective remained: "How comprehensive was his explanation?"
Although his position offered clarity regarding specific behavior, it reduced
the human experience to only what is observable. As we pursued more
philosophical topics, he maintained the same posture, as if the issues were
limited only to an observable dimension. Because of this, he did not address
my concerns. Skinner recreated the discussion around situations that characterized his thought. Skinner maintained that psychology as the science of
behavior must insist only upon a rigorous methodology, extending this
scientific analysis to a philosophical position. My perspective concerning the
implications of science for life was considerably different. I attempted to
propose and argue on behalf of my perspectives. However, we maintained the
points of view with which we began.)

Date: February, 1977

(As we continued, we talked about the underlying assumptions of his
work. In particular, we addressed his notions of truth that I suggested required
other than a scientific rationale. Although this interview shows some effort to
understand each other's apperceptions, each of us remained invested in
arguing his own position. To this, Skinner gave the following answer.)

BFS: A measure of truth is the degree to which you accept what is said and the
        degree to which that acceptance changes your life.
        That is no more an absolute truth than the truth of science.

Science is never absolutely true. I myself believe more in science than
revelation

but others, of course, disagree.

It all depends upon your private history and the extent to which these
things have come to modify your behavior.

(Our conversation explained how both Dr. Skinner and I maintained our
assumptions. I tried to relate to drawing upon his analysis of religion in
Science and Human Behavior [Skinner, 1953] and his personal evaluation of
faith. I anticipated that this might enable him to hear my epistemology.)

JC: Could you evaluate religion . . . without having experienced it?

BFS: I tend not to try to evaluate things in terms of how people feel.
I think we have overdone that; the Freudians have caused that.
It's what people now do because of this . . .

(Skinner had dismissed the role of feelings in life and staunchly refused to
entertain another perspective. He would not enter into another epistemology.)

JC: Can there be other ways of knowing, another epistemology which would
enable us to experience meaning as, for instance,
Kant speaks of it?
Kant says, for example, that knowing God is not possible for the natural
order because God is supernatural.
But he also points out that God provides man with the supernatural means
through prayer.
Could you not try to experience prayer to see if it does not change your
consciousness?

BFS: I really don't know what you're talking about.
I would like to see religion permit one to examine the world,
study it scientifically, without any threat that one is going to encounter
revealed truth.
My own belief about God is that we are on a very small planet around a
mediocre sun, which is one of billions of suns in our own galaxy and
there are billions of galaxies.
Now if God created all of that, who the devil are we to know anything
about him? I think it's ridiculous to suppose we can know God, and I
don't see why God should reveal anything to us.

(Although I felt I could understand his point, I did not believe that. From my view, he could not or would not address the faith and spiritual dimension of religion. At this point, our exchange began to stagnate because he resisted my efforts to draw him into my concerns. His resistance intensified my desire to pursue my interest.)

JC: What are you saying in terms of a supernatural power, then?
             In terms of God, what are you really saying?

BFS: Well, if God has revealed himself to us in different ways reported by
                  different religions
              and if I could choose one,
              I would obviously choose one because of my culture, my own history.

(Skinner held to his assumptions related to the empirical research reflected not only in his findings but also in the way he *interpreted* the findings.)

In this period of interviews, I tried to employ the language of behavioral analysis and did not defer to him, as I had in the previous interviews when he disagreed with an incompatible approach or concept. Within this polarized interaction, Dr. Skinner and I demonstrated different views that were not mutually shared or explored. We postured ourselves without regard to significant interaction or relationship, offering our own uncompromising perspectives. As interviewer, I proposed an antithetical position. As the polarized model suggests, I tended to characterize Dr. Skinner, based on his stance, as unaware and uninformed about faith. In the end, we were on different sides concerning the subject of motivation and religion. Where I valued religion, he seemed to trivialize religious experiences. Where he found behaviorism all-encompassing, I found behaviorism limiting.

I:R INTERVIEWING

In December of 1984, as I was rereading some of my correspondence with Dr. Skinner and felt that we had both shared important perspectives but had not come to grips with each other's point of view. I sent him a note that expressed my interest in discussing religion and science further. Dr. Skinner telephoned and said that he had read my note and would like to meet at my earliest convenience. He indicated that he was working on a book concerning ethics and behaviorism and felt that a discussion concerning religious issues and values might prove useful to him. We had different agendas and particular interests for this meeting, but I suggested that we speak freely about whatever issues came to our minds.

The interviews with Dr. Skinner followed a general pattern of discussion: limited structure, attentive listening, and pursuing the train of thought of both interviewee and interviewer. This permitted us to integrate our personal passions and ideas—the heart and mind—in our interview rather than to rely only upon predetermined questions that would direct the interview.

Because of our investment, we now may have been more attentive to one another. This time, the characteristics we shared, such as "truth-seeking," "independence," and "determination," resonated as points of contact. Such qualities brought us closer together and deepened our discussion. Skinner's yearnings as a utopian philosopher seemed to parallel my own spiritual quest; we were both convinced of the importance of empirical validation, and we both felt frustrated at hollow theories that did not demonstrate results. We agreed to meet weekly to pursue our concerns. These interviews continued from 1985 to 1990 and characterize the I:R approach.

Our interactive relationship led me to conclude how beneficial this work had been for the interviewing process, for permitting a deeper understanding of one another, and for the both of us personally. Selected segments from the multitude of tapes we recorded follow:

Date: December 29, 1986

JC: I would like to pursue the discussion of what is the "holy" to make clearer the point.

BFS: The attitudes are interesting, certainly.
What does it mean to be blessed?
I suppose it means . . . well, it could mean,
if you are blessed, either you behaved well and ought then to be
received by God,
or you have been given grace
and are to be received by God. They are supposed to be kept quite separate.
I've often wondered about this.
You . . . what is meekness—what do you do when you are meek?
You don't do anything!

JC: I think this relates very well to your work on cultural conditioning.
If, indeed, attitudes can be changed by a culture or faith, in addition to
improving the quality of life or leading one toward spiritual growth,

would we not be assuming or assisting "survival of the species," as you
put it?

BFS: Yes! Suppose a religion as a government is concerned about its
communicants who are suffering and need medical help.

Or, who are in need of food, and so on. If they can convince other rich
communicants or the intelligent ones to give, then they also require,

in addition to reinforcers used by the agency, some

self-reinforcing understanding of themselves as accepted by God or by all
people who admire people, and so on.

You certainly make a correction here . . . the poor will say, "Thank you,
God bless you;" and the "God bless you" is the return for giving—

and if you really believe that God is blessing you, then you are happy that
you are blessed.

And, I guess the point is: How much of that can go on before you do begin
to feel good about yourself the way other people feel towards you?

And, that would be some sense of,

well, very close to *agape,* certainly.

(Skinner's attunement shows itself through extending, where he researched words from my terminology (*agape*). He reciprocated my effort to
incorporate the language of behavioral analysis in my allusions. We entered
into each other's systems of thoughts; we defined aspects that concerned our
individual interests confirmed through each other's perspectives. Skinner
defined my usage of *agape* in the most truth-seeking terms he knew to
understand the value of "holiness"; I defined cultural conditioning in the
truth-seeking terms I knew to express appreciation for how his system could
achieve "holiness." In effect, we defended each other. I said people could reach
agape through cultural conditioning, and he said that people could reach *agape*
through religious behaviors.)

JC: That is an interesting point.

You know, you hear about relationships like that,

as you said, to being whole, being holy, to recalling that . . . the comfort of
a family, of a father, of a God, or connecting.

And, then, ultimately, is that a desirable way to be, theologically,
psychologically, and if you will, spiritually?

BFS: Well, I would certainly say that the God as a father or as a king, as a lord,
is all of those.

He is a king, a lord, and a father. And, for some people, the mother. And that, I think, could be traced to the effort of a religion as a government to fall back on standard forms of service to others.

JC: That's a helpful point. But through such discussion, I believe that it is helpful to distinguish *agape, philia,* and *eros* here again, and how the *experience* of them—not only in theory but in practice—let us understand how these experiences transform life itself.

BFS: Let's take the *agape* kind of thing, which I agree is very different from *philia* and *eros.*[2] . . .

I give you this quotation from someone,

"I love you means you reinforce me."

Somebody said that it is what a behaviorist would say. Well, of course, it is . . . however, it is true to love someone is to do good things for that person and to avoid doing harmful things.

Very importantly, the behavior of one who is loved is reinforced by the one who loves.

But the agape is the reverse of that.

You reach out and welcome someone who joins you—that's where I think it came from originally: the Greek word that goes back to another word meaning "welcome," "to take in."

If you show someone who joins you or joins your sect that you are pleased, then that reinforces the joining; it holds people together.

That is a reverse arrangement.

JC: But that is not adequately consistent with the notion of *agape* as demonstrated, let's say, with Jesus Christ.

Because Jesus was not establishing religion.

Let's look at *agape* and *philia* in the New Testament. Jesus says to Peter (John 21:15-17), "Do you love me?" In Greek, love here is translated as *agape.* Peter says, "Yes Lord, you know I love you." But here, Peter uses the Greek word *philia!*

This distinction is totally missing in the English.

Jesus repeats to Peter, "Do you love me?" Again, he asks if Peter has *agape* for him. Now in English, if this were merely repeating, this really makes no sense.

It's as if Jesus has a short-term memory problem.

But, of course, that's not the case; Peter simply isn't getting the point of the kind of love Jesus wants him to hear.

And, again, Peter answers, "You know that I love you. I have *philia* for you."
And I suppose Jesus understands and comes to be with Peter on Peter's
    terms by saying, "Peter do you love me?" (using *philia*)
Peter responds, "You know that I do."
And Jesus, from a nonreligious perspective, might sound as if he has a
    thought disorder, because after each response from Peter, he adds,
    "Feed" or "tend to my sheep." But actually he means, "it's all right that
    you have *philia* for me, but as you feed my sheep (behaviors, I might
    add), you will develop *agape!*"

(Our engagement had become consistent, resulting in a collaboration
around issues and ideas. For example, Skinner worked to understand
religion by researching the etymology of the term *agape*, identifying the
spiritual and behavioral dimensions. In turn, I interpreted the behavioral
component of a pericope that demonstrated how behaviors could lead to
agape.)

BFS: Yes, well, but do something for me.

JC: Not me, not me—that's the quantum leap, in a sense, of *agape*; it's to do it
          for "the other."

BFS: But whose sheep are they?

JC: I think the creation['s].
          You can feed "my sheep"—others.
          Let's go back to the text on that, of course.
          The sheep are the others.
          Jesus says, in essence, to Peter, I will be your friend—*philia*; but you must
              "feed the sheep,"—develop *agape*.
          And this is what changes us!

(Although we came to appreciate each other's perspective, we still tended
to interpret from the foundations we had established. Skinner focused on the
behavioral and concrete detail, feeding the sheep, while I focused on the
spiritual meaning. Skinner drew on this work for one of his publications;
[Skinner, 1989].)

JC: [Referring to the Gospel of Matthew] Do you recall the pericope where
          Christ is asked, "What do I need to do, Lord, in order to enter into
          heaven?"

BFS: Well, this is important because I think to love, worship, literally means "to note or clarify the work of someone." I worship God, I honor God, I bow down to God.

JC: You see, the reason again religion seems to be really significant to me is because it is the potential of a better state of being—a fuller state of being. In that sense, I am interested in religion.

And, I find that interest, believe it or not, supported by your approach on a number of levels.

In other words, when I look at religion, I look more at the person of Jesus Christ and His experience more than I do at religious people.

I don't perceive them as necessarily religious in that sense.

But, it is the *content,* again, of what He is doing which I consider critical action to experience life more fully, which I find energetic, powerful, and meaningful.

BFS: Feelings are simply by-products of the actual contingencies. Now what those contingencies are

would be whatever natural selection has contributed

to seeing your own while born,

cared for in infancy, and so on. . . .

Something that society reinforces [in] me, and I am sure that I have been reinforced when people have said, "You are very nice to your children."

(Although he became comfortable labeling his actions in terms of different kinds of loving behaviors, it appeared difficult for him to express the feelings of love. He responded in our discussions about love through further self-monitoring, observation, and description without exhibiting emotional involvement.)

JC: Now this is *philia* or *eros,* but now what of the *agape* toward man or God? Do you think you can have any genuine love or *agape* experience?

BFS: Now, when you say the religious experience, you mean the feelings people have when they talk about God?

JC: I would really be speaking about an encounter with God.

BFS: You mean an experience as the encounter—

"Do this and you will feel better, and so on,"

and if you can establish credibility,

people do feel better, and then you have power.

JC: But this perspective is born out of an insistence that everything is
  explained by utilitarianism and empiricism;
  it drains the mystical and awe from life and leaves everything dry.

BFS: I would say that the religious mystic's effort is to tell someone what it was
  like to feel—
  to receive—the grace of God . . .
  but I think it's nothing more than feelings after a positive event.

JC: So, [as Skinner previously detailed] an analysis of the young man who
  makes it through a plane crash, I think is interesting;
  you know, very, very helpful.
  He makes it, but the other guy doesn't make it.
  But, he says, "I'm saved, I'm something special, thank God, you know,
  God has given me grace."
  He feels special.

(In supporting the behavioral argument through self-disclosure, Skinner
reported a historical fact and shared the impact of the event.)

BFS: Well, I did hear that, you know, when I found a watch.

(Skinner, here, referred to a watch that he lost as a child. He prayed and
then found the watch. He saw this now as mere coincidence.)

  That was a "high." I mean, God has *done* something.

JC: Now, first, I think that faith is more than this. The spiritual attitude is a
  different kind of excitement. . . .
  Religious people who genuinely try to embrace an attitude of faith, hope,
  love . . . always try to display, if you will, that "high."

BFS: Well, I would . . .
  this all comes down, I think, to what kind of contingencies we want people
  to live under.
  And I would like to see people enjoy their work, for example.
  And they do, how they might not say, "Oh! I had a great high today; I had
  a wonderful time; things came out very well," and so on.
  But it is so much better than the adverse control of the worker. . . .
  See, money is not a reinforcer . . . ordinary wages.
  It's something you give that you can take away by firing somebody.
  You don't work for wages; you work to avoid losing them.

(We not only affirmed each other's perspectives and learned about each other's background, we built a new space and established a new relationship that allowed us to challenge and confront one another intensely. Our responses appeared free of defense and were given in an open and thoughtful manner, as evidenced by the disclosure of further information.)

JC:　Then how do you understand love for others?

BFS:　It is all based on *eros,* certainly it's based on *keratas* (charity), too, I
　　　　should think.

　　　　My love for other people, I would say, would probably be more *agape* and
　　　　eros than *philia.*

　　　　Philia, to me, is like love of music, love of art, love of what I do,
　　　　my work,
　　　　and so forth.

　　　　A strong, positive inclination to do the kinds of things that I do.
　　　　I love doing those.
　　　　I love a pleasant day.
　　　　I love walking each morning, and so on.

JC:　I don't know that that's *agape.* Do you think you have had enough faith (not
　　　　only religious) experience to really evaluate what are spiritual matters?

BFS:　There was always a certain element of fear. Not exactly that I might have
　　　　the wrong religion . . . be a Presbyterian instead of a Catholic . . . but
　　　　that I was not really religious.

JC:　But do you think the quality of your experience misses *agape,* awe, or
　　　　relationship?

BFS:　I guess I would make a distinction between "form" and "content."

(This was something I had asked him to do some 17 years earlier—to distinguish content and form. Because we experienced a new relationship through concepts such as attunement, attending, and extending, we could hear each other deeply and with understanding.)

Date: December 18, 1987

BFS:　I'm talking about whether there is a parallel in natural selection for all of
　　　　this. Certainly, in the evolution of eating, escaping,
　　　　the evolution of doing things with living creatures,
　　　　the evolution of grooming—and apes groom each other,

and I assume that it's pleasant to them being groomed,
and so on. Those are quite—
in a way—quite parallel,
except for the time scale of when they were acquired,
which took millions of years,
to the things that I've learned to do.
Where I've learned to eat well,
by looking carefully both ways, and so on;
how I get to know people
and how I behave in order to have people say,
"I saw you on television and you were wonderful,"
and so on, and so on.
These are the things that I have acquired as an individual.
Certainly, there was a good deal of this in my natural history, as well,
I think.

JC: And, see, this is a very important discussion for our work because of the
        following:
in my mind, that is,
you're saying that I don't know if there is importance in the order of
        different reinforcement. That is
that, as Maslow suggests,
a hierarchy of values or order where there are reinforcements of survival
needs, safety needs, love needs, esteem needs, and self-actualization.
But it's precisely that certain individuals in the order that sets up
        implications for the nature,
or the understanding of nature, of human personality because . . .

BFS: What do we gain by noticing the needs or order. . . .
I think it's just a question of ability.
A plant . . . a seed sprouts. It can't photosynthesize yet till it's got some
        leaves, and so on.

(Here, Dr. Skinner's tone shows his reflective process and wondering in contrast to his authoritative restatement. His inquisitive manner seeking truth invites the potential for action. I listened to Dr. Skinner talk in order to generate the associations necessary to engage more direction in our discussion. Unlike our earlier interviews, characterized as monolithic and polarized, our determination here did not dominate the other's viewpoint but, instead, achieved a common base from which we could work together. We both sought the elements of truth present in each other's views. These points of contact resonated and deepened our investment and heightened our attunement and attentiveness. Subsequently, we could relate with greater openness, or authenticity, without defending as if our beliefs were attacked.)

JC: That's [nurturance is] very important.

(Energizing pulse is engaged.)

JC: Let me try to make the last point by referring to a young man I saw in prison yesterday.
This 19-year-old came from a very established, seemingly model home, yet he is imprisoned for assault and battery and robbery. He is a bright and sensitive fellow,
but he was not adequately nurtured.
The last point is that after we have established the self-esteem, after, let's say, B. F. Skinner has a sense of his self, his productivity, his writing, his sense of achievement as an individual, which assumes that all of the other needs are met: food, safety, love . . .

BFS: I can say, after B. F. Skinner has been flattered, and so on and so on, his behavior from having acquired a sense of worth or self-esteem, and so on.
See, I want to get rid of the individual.
And that is apparently what the Eastern religions have done, although I haven't been able to follow them very closely. That's what a great many religious people have tried to do.
It's the annihilation of the self.

(Even though Skinner's interruption appears to change the course of my comment, his association attempts to meet me in my sphere of influence concerning religion and reveals more about his person. In the interviews characterized by the other models, Skinner presented himself as antireligious, even atheistic. Here, he emerged as considering, perhaps even appreciating, religious goals. In return, I attended to his insights within his sphere of influence pertaining to psychological concerns.)

JC: And that's why I feel, with regard to this thinking, as it were, that the Christian mode of thinking that I have been trying to compare with your work—

that there is some sensitivity to . . . both the individual and the social order
and scientific reality.

BFS: I was impressed by one thing: that Eastern Orthodoxy,
as contrasted with Roman Catholicism, is going for a felt state rather than
rules.

(Here Skinner reciprocates attunement by confirming an aspect of my
own faith—Eastern Orthodox.)

BFS: And that's why what you say does not sound like religion—
that if you don't have the hope, and so on . . .
and its . . .
and that seems to me very closely tied up with what I have been working
on the last year or two.
I'm sure that our conversations have contributed to it.

(Skinner demonstrated attending and extending through affirming my
faith, identifying with our work, and showing how our work influenced his
academic endeavors. We could enter each other's spheres of influence with
greater ease, increasing the understanding of each other's positions, and
seemingly defending each other's point of view. We continued our conversation over lunch.)

In 1988, I visited B. F. Skinner at the hospital the day following his brain
surgery. As I entered the room at Massachusetts General Hospital, he was
surrounded by his daughters and wife. Upon recognizing me, he looked up
and said,

> I knew that if I were to get out of this alive, you would ask me how I was *feeling*
> before my surgery. I kept thinking about our discussions, asking myself such
> questions as they rolled me down the corridor into the surgery room. Well, I
> don't think I felt anything. I don't think I was afraid to die and don't remember
> wanting to pray, but I'm glad to wake up!

I was struck by how personally our work had affected him. On the brink
of death, he wrestled with the questions that we had tirelessly argued as he
self-monitored his reactions. Acknowledging my surprise, he quipped, "You
needn't worry. We can still continue to talk about things. Those cognitive
psychologists were not successful in using this opportunity, when they bore
holes into my skull, to change my thoughts." We laughed.

Our interviews demonstrated the I:R model. We explored, wondered, and reflected on one another's thoughts. Although this set of interviews began with a particular topic, it evolved into an exchange of thoughts, ideas, and even feelings. Drawing on personal characteristics, we engaged the potential for action, deepened our understanding of one another, and developed a new relationship.

The I:R Model:
A Comparative Discussion

My interviews with B. F. Skinner reflect three different models of interaction. These three models provide three distinct impressions of him. The first interview exemplified the monolithic model. I viewed B. F. Skinner as a towering authority; he spoke and I listened. I found him impenetrable, stolid, and emotionally distant. As a result, the interaction presented only one voice because neither of us understood the other.

The second interview exemplified the polarized model. I experienced B. F. Skinner as limited in his experience and understanding of religion, arrogant in his thinking about approaches different from his own, and emotionally aloof. Although I deeply respected his facile thinking and wished to know more about his views, we offered different perspectives and both ended up fairly close to where we started—maintaining our own points of view.

The third set of interviews demonstrated the I:R model. Here, Dr. Skinner and I left the comfort of our own worldviews and ventured to thinking through the other's perspective. As a result, both of us changed—if not our basic values, certainly our thoughts. I came to appreciate the behavioral critique of religious activity; he learned about and incorporated concepts about faith that transcend religious practices and take into consideration spiritual realities. We delighted in conversations that provided enhanced meaning through our shared perspectives, such as in the example of the analysis of different kinds of love.

The transcription of the three models from Dennis Tedlock's proposal for translation reveals how both B. F. Skinner and I became more thoughtful and reflective in our responses in the I:R model. Whereas well-rehearsed scripts may typify interviews where interviews are not challenged or engaged (in the monolithic and polarized models), the I:R interview illustrates more pauses, a process of rethinking and reshaping thought.

In the long series of interviews that I believe characterize the I:R approach, I experienced B. F. Skinner as a truth-seeking scientist and reflective man. If I had not had the opportunity to interview through the I:R approach, I would not have understood him as deeply. In a period of more than 5 years, I observed his unusual ability to persevere in his work, to express care for others in terms of visionary planning, and to apply his theory in his own life. The I:R approach enabled me to understand and communicate with him, and it also enabled him, in turn, to do the same with me. Although I found him extraordinarily regimented in his life and restrained in his emotional experiences, he honestly portrayed himself and his work.

At one juncture, I told Dr. Skinner that I found his approach to life and values spiritual. He valued the good and tried to live accordingly. He responded with satisfaction, stating that previous to our work, he would not have considered issues of his concern as spiritual. The word *spiritual* had a mystical, silly ring to it for him. He became more comfortable with mature notions of faith. Much to the surprise of many viewers, he acknowledged his sensitivity to spirituality from our work in a Public Broadcasting System (PBS) interview.

The progression in the models reflects changes in the interview concerning posturing, characteristics, and skills. As shown in this chapter, the models mirror the dynamics that I brought as interviewer. As a result, this reflected my approach and ultimately affected the image that I developed of Skinner. Therefore, our ability to see the interviewee is often limited by our own posturing.

The models reviewed in this chapter showed the ways interviews have occurred in traditional approaches and the progression toward the I:R approach. As demonstrated, an interview may include aspects of more than one model. Additionally, one need not move developmentally or successfully through each model to experience the I:R approach. Neither do these models require significant periods of time to acquire.

In the next chapter, you will read about the interviews I conducted with Lucille Ball. As you read, consider the following:

1. How might your qualities have affected the course of the interview?
2. As I have previously stated, one could conduct the following interview with a list of prearranged questions. How might that have affected the interview?
3. Ultimately, an interview should lead to a comprehensive understanding of an individual. As you read, do you think the personal characteristics used in this

approach enabled us to learn more about Lucille Ball than a traditional, formal approach?

As the interview unfolds, consider your responses and thoughts to the previous questions. In addition to identifying how personal characteristics affected the course of the interview, I highlight various aspects of the I:R approach.

Notes

1. I wish to acknowledge the contribution of William R. Rogers (see Christine Brusselman's [1980] *Toward Moral and Religious Maturity*), whose diagrams concerning the interdisciplinary dialogue of religion and psychology inspired my effort to conceptualize interviewing postures diagramatically.

2. In our discussion about love, we distinguished three variations of the term *love* in Greek, correlating this word with behavioral and psychoanalytic applications: *eros,* or "desire" in Greek, with natural selection (behaviorism) or the libido or id (psychoanalysis); *philia,* or "friendship" in Greek, with operant conditioning or action of the individual (behaviorism) or the ego (psychoanalysis); and *agape,* or "unconditional love" in Greek, with cultural conditioning or the community's ability to give rise to behaviors that benefit the group (behaviorism) or the super ego (psychoanalysis). Note that Dr. Skinner and I did not confirm the equivalency of these parallels but found the distinctions helpful for discussing the foci of these various perspectives.

5

Interviewing and the
Interactive-Relational Approach

This chapter identifies and explains the ways in which a full expression of the interaction and the relationship through the previously identified components result in an inner view. The chapter presents segments from the initial meeting with Lucille Ball that demonstrate the impact of the interactive-relational (I:R) approach in a journalistic interview setting. In this interview, we observe how the personal characteristics of openness, nurturance, and respect resonate with Lucy and how expressed personal characteristics can advance an I:R interview.

Lucille Ball: An I:R Encounter

In Lucille Ball, I met a living legend. Her talent and on-screen projection of accessibility and warmth made her respected by millions around the world.

This image made me feel as though I had personally known her before meeting her.

Why did Ms. Ball gain such access to so many people in so many different cultures? How did her life experiences equip her to touch people in this way? What were the differences between this icon of society and the person? Unsure of what to expect, I held an idealized notion of Ms. Ball, as her shows entertained me during my childhood and adulthood. In contrast, magazine articles and talk shows painted her as a callous, demanding, and shrewd businesswoman.

On the day of our first meeting, when I arrived at Ms. Ball's mansion, she answered the door herself and greeted me with an outstretched hand. She wore simple dark slacks and a light blue blouse. Her renowned red hair was offset by a pair of large, dark sunglasses. She moved with the ease that one would not ordinarily associate with someone in her 70s. She exuded warmth. In her low, raspy voice, she invited me to join her in the living room.

As we sat and engaged in small talk, I wondered which of the comic disguises characterized her true nature best: the zany hysterical housewife? the ballerina? the matador? the martian? the grape stomper? the statue? the hillbilly? Before we began discussion, she invited, "Please call me Lucy."

At this point, I realized that our casual conversation enhanced our rapport. Although opening my notes on the end table, I sat back and continued to engage in the friendly discussion. We both initiated topics ranging from my West Coast trips to her children and daily life. Some of this dialogue was central to the interview before recording our conversation. Some of our conversation led us into issues that I planned to explore in the formal interview. However, I felt that I was getting to know her better through this unplanned discussion more than the organized interview format I had pre-pared. Although still not having begun the formal interview, Lucy escorted me through her yard and garden. We stopped and talked at the pool and the guest house as I inquired about her daily routine. We recalled some of her antics from her shows. During our walk, she told me about her love for games like Scrabble and backgammon, as well as for most sports. She lamented about not being on the set for a show.

The initial engagement reflected casual conversation. This allowed us to become comfortable with each other and, significantly, provided both of us the opportunity to *experience* the encounter. This encouraged rapport and ascertained basic information about each other's character.

As we began to talk about my project, she lit up a cigarette—a topic of another conversation—and expressed how honored she felt to take part in my book on outstanding American women. Suddenly, she commented, "You know, I feel really comfortable with you; so why am I wearing these sunglasses?" With that delightful frown, she remarked, "They don't hide the wrinkles, anyway." We laughed as she removed them. I felt several things at her disclosure. First, I was surprised that she felt the need to hide her wrinkles. Second, I felt reassured that she felt comfortable enough with me to set aside her vanity. Given our rapport, I thought this was a good time to begin the formal interview. However, I would not move systematically through questions. Instead, I chose to maintain our personal connection and interweave the questions within our discussions. Placing the recorder on "play," we just began to talk.

Selected sections of my initial meeting with Lucy follow and demonstrate some of the turns that happen in the I:R approach. I transcribed this verbatim account using Dennis Tedlock's (1988) method for translation. As noted earlier regarding Tedlock's approach, the beginning of a new line in transcription indicates the speaker's pause in order to demonstrate original or reflective thinking rather than patented responses. In the following verbatims, such pauses often highlight new thoughts in Lucy's response. In addition, I have included text in parentheses to reflect logistical directions, my thoughts during the interview, or an explanation of the interview process.

LB = Lucille Ball
JC = John Chirban
Date: April 15, 1982

LB: Oh God, one of those old *bios*. Not even true, half of it.

(The bios were accurate. I could not tell if Lucy tried to make me feel comfortable, felt embarrassed by seeing that I held her portfolio, or was simply modest, so I asked:)

JC: Is that so? (I laughed.)

(I chose to believe that this reflected her humility.)

LB: Yeah.
JC: Okay.

(I respected her drive to portray the biographical information according to her desire. However, I would need to revisit the facts in the interest of truth.)

LB: I'll correct what is . . . what isn't.

(She really suggested that things about her had been overstated.)

JC: Thank you.

(So, I began the interview. Based on our interaction together, I elected to forego the structured interview I had planned. I allowed the relational aspect of our rapport to guide me in tailoring the queries by providing Lucy with open-ended questions.)

JC: How would you describe your career?
LB: I certainly don't resent it.
          I adore it. God, if I wasn't an entertainer, I don't know what I would like to
          be.
JC: Because also you're sometimes considered a businesswoman.

(I said this as if reminding her. I had two images of Lucy; in one, she held the role of warmly humorous comedian, and in the other, hardened business-woman. Our rapport had begun to develop as we spoke during our walk. We had already begun to share, and I found her very pleasant. I considered this an opportunity to address my confusion.)

LB: Not if you really knew me.

(She was surprised by my comment and responded in disbelief.)

JC: Okay.

(In responding this way, I intended to allow her to elaborate. Most interview-ers might seek to develop the point. However, I tried to convey openness and respect. My tone invited Lucy to elaborate on herself, to engage the potential for action. Although very early into the interview, she experienced my openness, respect, and nurturance, qualities that she valued, and that I recog-nized in her. She responded in kind, which continually deepened the inter-view. This interview demonstrates rapid movement through the first and second stages of I:R.)

LB: I was not,
uh,
that was something I inherited,
and, uh,
didn't take much pleasure in.
I don't like hiring and firing.
I'm *rather*
good at personnel,
uh,
you know,
judging a,
a character here and there and making the right decision.
But, uh,
I was never a great businesswoman, and it took me 7 years to stop heading up the three studios and get rid of them and get my small company back where I felt comfortable.

(At this point, I was struck by the pauses she made and her unassuming attitude. I felt as if she wanted me to come to her aid by her reflection and the quizzical expression on her face. I put my questionnaire down and pursued her disclaimer of hardened businesswoman.)

JC: In some of the things that have been written about you that I've read—
and I'm just trying to recall—
they've said,
at least some writers have said, that you're a very shrewd and solid businesswoman.
Is that . . .
LB: Well, I think,
uh,
some writers,
oh, you mean,
uh.
JC: Like,
like articles . . .

(I attuned to her desire to engage my help and to identify the source of this characterization.)

LB: People writing books.

JC: Or books.

LB: Well, uh, it,
it seems that way because I had three studios
and five thousand people that worked for me,
and,
or more or less,
and, uh,
it covered a period 7 or 8 years,
and they also didn't believe that I didn't do any of,
of the business work—
when I,
when Desi and I were associated.
They just took for granted that
that I did do a lot of it.
I did nothing!
I had babies, and I went to work and enjoyed my work
and went home
and took care of the home.
But they never believed it
because he was a
a Cuban bandleader, and they just didn't think that he—
He *proved* it, though!
They know *now.*
They know now that he was a *great* businessman.
And, uh,
but we were in at the very beginning
and it, uh,
it was incongruous. They didn't even want him to be
on my show as my husband, although he was. We had to prove *that.*
That part of the biog is right.
But, uh,
when I,
by the time I inherited the studios,
there was a lot I didn't know, but I had a lot of *very* trustworthy
uh
influential

uh

men that had been with us for several years,

and that meant a *lot* to me.

I learned a lot and I had to make a final decision, *yes,*

but it was sort of handed to me on a platter, I still have those men

in doing my business affairs,

but I did inherit the studios,

uh. . . .

Well,

I wasn't such a nincompoop.

I did . . .

(I listened to her through adapting appropriate microskills and attentive body language that expressed interest. This seemed to enable her to respond more quickly. Immediately, she seemed to relive her feelings about misunderstandings concerning Desi.)

JC: You were skeptical—

LB: I was more skeptical, uh, as far as—I don't know, I'm not speaking about husbands particularly or men or women in general, but I got down to business.

I had to.

But, uh, as far as getting *hardened,*

uh,

they hadn't seen me do anything but have fun on the set,

I guess, or just work.

They just assumed that if I was up there, running board meetings and being with lawyers, that I must have, uh, changed in some way.

They didn't know how frightened I was and how much I depended on some very honest men.

That are still with me.

(I had concerns that we had begun to touch on some very personal topics and that a pursuit of this matter would disrupt our rapport. More importantly, I felt drawn to attend to her feelings. I also felt that the interview might get too intense, too fast, which I feared could work against it. I decided to leave this subject and return to more neutral issues. This situation reflects both characteristics of respect and nurturing and developing a relationship to achieve its

intended end. Later in the interview, Lucy explained that no one was there
"to protect her." Interestingly, she pulled for protection—she responded to
it—perhaps in the same way she kept the "very honest men" around her, as
she repeated twice. My sense is that my respect and nurturing felt protective
to her—and so she came forth even more. In this process of the interview, she
felt my care.)

> **JC:** Mm, hm.
> From what the bio said, again,
> you took a pretty critical turn at 15, trying to make it in show business.
> **LB:** Well, I left, uh . . .
> **JC:** Jamestown.

(Knowledge of the interviewee's history enhances her confidence in the
seriousness of the interviewer. Careful preparation strengthens the sense that
the interviewer knows the interviewee, thereby encouraging greater sharing.)

> **LB:** Jamestown (she smiled) and went back to dramatic school
> lasted one
> short summer season, and they literally wrote a letter and said my mother was
>   wasting her money.
> It was a, that's true
> and uh,
> I-I-I
> don't know and rightly so because,
> I-I was so reticent.
> I never opened my mouth, and when I did
> I said all the wrong things. And
> I sounded
> real horses and water
> and I don't know whether that's Middle Western or
> we weren't from the Middle West, but I-I
> was very
> mostly I was
> I was
> shy and terrified
> absolutely terrified of New York City. I didn't, uh, dare walk on the streets.
> And I-I didn't enjoy it.
> I wanted to be part of the business.

I wanted to take

uh,

dancing and singing and dramatics.

And I went to the John Murrey Anderson Robert Milton Dramatic School.

And it was a proper Milton diction elocutionist who said,

"Mm, there's no way with this girl. She just sounds terrible, and she's
   awkward." I couldn't walk across the,

I was so frightened.

I got over it after I became a model.

Modeling helped me quite a bit,

and from modeling I only,

my only bit of show business I *ever ever* got was 5 weeks of rehearsal,

and then tossed out on some show—

I've forgotten what it was—

and, uh,

finally got into show business by coming out here on a fluke,

really,

for 6 weeks, and the 6 weeks

never stopped.

I've never been out of work except for 3 hours.

That's why I've always been so satisfied.

It sounds like I came up the *hard* way, but to me it was *marvelous* to be paid
   a lot of money after getting 25 dollars and 35 dollars a week to suddenly
   get hundreds of dollars a week to be learning a business.

It's a great way to apprentice.

JC: Then the entertainment profession you describe is really tough.

LB: You have to.

You can't say, Oh, it's, uh, the most you can say is,

if I made it anybody can, because I had no talents whatsoever.

I have never studied for anything.

I hadn't even finished school.

So the most—that's the,

that's the best I can say. And now there's more

competition—harder to get into the unions, harder to get recognition—
   because of the great competition,

and you even get a job, and get into a series, and the series cancels after

3 weeks, and you got to start all over.

And you have to live with rejection.

But I said I don't want to sit here and talk about rejection. I just want to mention it and forget it.

(It was apparent that the mere term "rejection" disturbed her.)

JC: Mm hm.
LB: I want to talk about all the things that you should be
JC: doing.

(At this point, it became apparent to me that Lucy was prepared to discuss concrete actions and facts but not to reveal the intensity of her passions and pains through a discussion of feelings. My attunement to her thought and language enabled me to communicate with her—and eventually address the feelings about things that she avoided or denied.)

LB: . . . doing.
JC: . . . to make your salary.
LB: To, uh,
    let you eat.
JC: Right.
LB: Because you don't prostitute yourself.
JC: Right.
LB: If you are able to eat and put a shirt on your back, then you don't go out
    and do some pornographic junk and wish you hadn't.
JC: Mm hm.
LB: Times are changing, wrong to prostitute and-and-and you've got to know
    that it's still wrong to prostitute yourself.
JC: What?

(The direction Lucy had taken caused me to wonder. Was this issue moralistic or personal?)

LB: In any way.

(She was so amazingly unaware of her hard work; she was self-effacing and seemingly guilt-ridden. I wondered if Lucy did not understand her own talent, and that turmoil lay beneath her responses. As a result of our discussions to this point, I decided to ask a question that would assume that she had gone through hard times to see if I could learn about the forces in her life.)

JC: Who was giving the warm hand or the-the support and the comfort through
          the confusing days of waiting in line and not getting . . .

(I drew from my perception of her need to feel caring in the form of protection.
This was my response to her, not a conscious effort to draw her out. Her desire
for protection resonated with my desire to nurture. This engaged the potential
for action. In my efforts to nurture her, I noted her difficulty with expressing
feelings directly. In concrete action images, such as a warm hand, I presented
scenarios to connect caring. This attunement of her needs struck a chord on
which she resonated but initially denied and discussed later in the interview.)

LB: No.

JC: . . . appointments. There wasn't anyone?

LB: I ran away from Celeron,
          which is a suburb of Jamestown,
          and I packed my bag and hiked to New York. And then I got so
          homesick, I was visibly ill.
          Have you ever been homesick?

(I nodded affirmatively. Lucy attempted to make sure that I understood her
and could relate to her. She sought my reassurance.)

LB: It's a terrible illness.
          I mean really sick. You cry, you can't eat, and you just gotta get home.
          So I'd take my last nickel and put it in the telephone. I'd reverse the charges
              and say, "Mom, I gotta come home." I used to get very, very homesick
              because there wasn't anything that wrong at home.
          But at the same time, I was just *dying* to get into the business,
          but no,
          no that's why I got so homesick and-and wanted to come home.
          I could stand New York just a very short time.
          And then I had to get out.
          I was so terrified of everybody . . .

JC: Really.

LB: and I was terrified of the girls.
          I felt I was getting *showgirl*. I was making the interviews, making the
              auditions.

JC: Mm hm.

(Although minimal encouragers [Ivey et al., 1993] such as "mm, hm," "OK," and "right" may not seem insightful, they facilitate a sense of the interviewer's presence, attention, and support.)

LB: but, uh,

JC: Yes.

LB: I wasn't keeping the jobs. I was so terrified of the showgirls
that I,
that I couldn't talk.
They were all very tough, rough, bawdy, frightening
I think I'll remember that all my life,

JC: Mm hm.

LB: and I think I have had compassion for beginners because of that.

JC: But who was present in your walk? In other words, there wasn't someone
along with you, saying, "Come on, Lucy, you're doing great?" With all
the support and all that?

(I had a hard time understanding why she had been so much alone, so I searched to learn more detail. Through the probing, new avenues for connection emerged. This ignited the potential for action where my offering of respect, openness, and nurturant characteristics resonated with her responsiveness to such care. I wondered if this could have made her seem so vulnerable yet so strong. In a sober and calm way, she responded:)

LB: No, there wasn't anyone around.
I didn't know anyone.
I didn't go anyplace. I never—

(With most of the achieved women who I interviewed, there had been a female who had taken extraordinary interest in that woman's life, so I asked again:)

JC: But there wasn't necessarily an aunt and mother that was showing that
kind of

LB: no

JC: . . . uh,
walking with you and that

LB: no

JC: Mm, hm, okay.

LB: No, there never was; there wasn't anyone available.

(At this point, her servant interrupted our interview with drinks and snacks. Lucy digressed, discussing the news and asking questions about what board games I liked to play. This gave me a view about her style and sensitivities. Lucy engaged comfortably in personal discourse with me, and I began to speak to her about her life with Desi.)

JC: How have you responded to, to failure? We began speaking about that in
   terms of your first marriage.
   But how have you handled that, assuming . . .

LB: As quietly as possible . . .

JC: Mm hm.

LB: comes to mind first.

JC: Right.

LB: I didn't talk about it.
   It, it wasn't, that I wasn't facing it.
   I was facing it alone.
   I talked about it to my mother.
   I really didn't know the things that I know now
   and have learned
   since . . . I didn't know how I was being cheated on, and

JC: Mmm.

LB: uh . . . what people really thought, until much later. My brother knew
   things that he didn't tell me. He traveled on the road with Desi. And he
   didn't tell me anything until after I got a divorce. I said, "Why didn't
   you tell me?" He said, "Well, sis, I didn't want to make you unhappy.
   You know. . . ."

JC: Yes.

LB: "I always thought things might work out, and, and then when you got into
   television things seemed so much better."

JC: But you also implicitly suggest that that kind of lifestyle was not
   acceptable to you. In other words,

LB: Never! (Affirming my observation.)

JC: There are people, nowadays, who are open to so-called open marriage.

LB: Nowadays (lifting her eyebrow).

JC: Right.

(I wanted to find out whether Lucy made any accommodation in her beliefs for the overpublicized loose morals of Hollywood.)

LB: Not then, and, uh,
certainly not for me.

JC: And not for you.

LB: OK.

JC: That was not your idea of what the family should be like.

LB: Hell, no!

JC: I see.

LB: No, he cheated on me from the first month we were married.

JC: And that was unacceptable.

LB: *Very.*
But you begin to think it's your fault. And you're
Not sure. You, you think, I . . .

JC: The cause.

LB: I'm jealous.
I'm, I'm
I've got, I've got a lot of work to do on myself, and I worked on,
I couldn't find any answers.

JC: Uh, huh.

LB: And I thought, well this is not all in my mind. He never admitted anything.
That was one of the . . .

JC: Difficult parts.

(In offering to complete her thought, I did not feel that I led the interview or her responses. Instead, I felt that I understood and reflected her agony, which enabled her to share her deeper emotions.)

LB: I don't know, maybe it was better that he didn't?
He was taught never to admit,
which seems to be a Latin
dogma.

JC: Mm hm.

LB: His father said, "Even if you're caught in bed with someone, deny it. And you'll find that sooner or later they'll say, 'Well, maybe, I didn't see that.' "

(We laughed.)

JC: May I ask you why you "terminated" with Desi?

(The humor, however, sharply halted as Lucy reflected on her inner thoughts. She began to cry:)

LB: Desi did everything,
and nothing in moderation.

(long pause)

I had it all—*booze, broads,* and *gambling.*
It sounds vulgar.

(Again, Lucy found it easier to describe the actions of unpleasant events rather than her feelings directly. However, shifting my attention to her descriptors—speaking her language and not forcing language about feelings—Lucy heard my questions and eventually responded with feelings. The present orientation of the interview brought the intensity of her emotions to the surface.)

. . . but that's what it was.

(Crying, she continued.)

And we've talked about it, and I've said it before.
JC: Mmm.
LB: . . . and I just couldn't tolerate it anymore.
And when the children got to an age where they were asking questions, uh, I
got fed up with saying, "Daddy isn't feeling well."
He just would not take care of himself,
and he never honored our marriage.
He still loves *us,*
but, uh, he plays around.
And, uh,
it was, took me a long time to realize it was a lost cause,
'cause we stayed married 19 years. But the last 6 years,
it was
just sort of
finishing our commitments, businesswise.

(I was moved by her genuine poignant emotion. It was still quite a live drama for her. To a woman who held commitment in such high regard, Lucy felt devastated by living a duplicitous lifestyle.)

JC: As I hear you speak, there's also a sound or tone of care and love in your voice about him. Would you say that's accurate?

(Because Lucy felt understood, she now could respond to my question about feelings directly. Lucy appeared to fit the stereotype of comedienne, not having access to negative affect. Nevertheless, our new relationship allowed us to penetrate this well-honed defense.)

(Still crying . . .)

LB: Yes, uh,
          care
          and understanding

(By her deep emotional response to past events, she confirmed, in part, my impression that she still had feelings for Desi, that she still felt love.)

          That's the way he is.
JC: Mm hm.
LB: He's, uh, still that way.
          (sipping her drink and lighting a cigarette)
          And I didn't want the children,
          and I didn't have, I didn't want to have to explain to the children as they grew up. They found out for themselves . . .

(clearing throat)

          Pardon me . . .
          that there was, was not exactly the way to go.
          I think they've learned.
JC: And there were only two children?
LB: Yep, I lost two, and had two—
JC: Oh, I didn't know that.
LB: I was pretty *busy* there for 5 years.
JC: Right.
LB: I had children very late in life, making you appreciate them more.

> Keeps you young
> 'cause, he was on the road,
> and he was in the army
> 3½ years, and then after he got back was on the road 5 years. We'd been married 9 years and been together about *7 months.*

JC: Mm hm.

LB: You can't have children long distance.

JC: Right.

LB: So, finally, he got off the road and stopped drinking
> for a year and then I got pregnant.
> I lost the first two, and then I had two.

(Lucy described one emotional trauma after another. She visibly expressed hurt but seemed confessional. Her unusual personal strengths came through in her personal story.)

LB: Lucie's (referring to her daughter) a new mother.

JC: Is it her first?

LB: Yes.

JC: Congratulations.

LB: Thank you; he's *adorable!*

JC: Oh, that must be fun for you.

LB: He's *sensational!* . . .
> I have to show you my pictures before you go.

JC: Please. And how old is he now?

LB: 16 months.

JC: Oh. That's fun.
> So you're watching him grow?

LB: Oh, yes.

JC: And his name?

LB: Simon Luckinbill.

(I paused. Upon hearing the name, I pictured an old man not consistent with an adorable infant. Lucy detected my countertransference and responded. Transference and countertransference are not points of contact of authentic selves but images in the minds of the participants. Transference and counter-transference disconnect the genuine relationship. It is striking to observe how Lucy reengaged our contact. She tried to understand my reaction and resonate with my discomfort to the name Simon. Such attunement demonstrated her reciprocity.)

LB: Simon Thomas Luckinbill.

(Because I did not respond, she worked vigorously to reengage me. She became highly attuned to my feelings and, through her response, expressed her desire to reestablish the connection that we had developed.)

JC: Why?
LB: Well, she was doing "They're Playing Our Song," written by Neil Simon.
          She thought it was a nice name
          I guess.

(In this case, because of her effort to maintain our connection, my countertransference enabled Lucy to share more. She now resonated my feelings about the name to maintain our engagement and continued to offer more information.)

          I do too,
          now. It frightened me at first I said. "*Simon,*

(We both laughed. This laugh confirmed the "repair" to our rift in communications set off by my countertransference.)

          Where did you get Simon?"
          Nobody in the family is named Simon. . . .
          But I *love* it now!

(Following a break in the interview and a discussion about my academic work that she initiated, we returned to our discussion of family mishaps.)

JC: How do you handle the sadness?
LB: I? What can I do about it? I go ahead and do. If there's nothing to be done
          about it, I don't dwell on it.
JC: Okay.
LB: And I try to comfort the people that it—it affects directly.
JC: What principles guide your life? What would you say are the most
          important principles for you?
LB: (sigh) Well, early on—

now I'm sure I'm answering this correctly—
my principles . . .
I've always been very honest. But early on I had to learn to like myself and
    do something that I admired whether it was just get home in a straight line
    or get in and out of the office—having taken, been rejected, or whatever—
and still live through it. Because, I, when it first happened to me, I wanted to
    commit suicide.
But I was very careful—I was going to get hit by a limousine, not just an old
    car. I was a dreamer but, uh . . .

(Lucy had not moved beyond the discussion of Desi, here, as she referred to
"rejection." I had the sense that the same was true in her life. Lucy recomposed
herself.)

JC: Do you find the task of being an entertainer tough? Is it that difficult—

(Although I could have continued with this theme of Desi, I felt compassion
and respect and thought to pursue so as to allow Lucy to hold her composure.)

LB: No.

JC: Mm hm.

LB: I love it!
It's not been tough at all. Uh,
There have been times when, when you worked beyond your physical
    strength.

JC: Mm hm.

(Lucy's denial of her difficulties glared through.)

LB: I found it very tough in "Wildcat." . . .
The only task that I remember was trying to live with the humility—
the, uh, humiliation, rather—

JC: Mmm.

LB: of my marriage.

JC: This is going to be almost like a return to something we've talked about,
    but I think it's important.
It's sometimes said that for women who achieve vocational fulfillment there's
    an emotional loss. Is this true for you?

LB: Been like the opposite for me.

I don't know what I would have done if if I hadn't gone into the business.
I love show business.
I love show business.

(Lucy interpreted my question as if I were asking about her fulfillment as an entertainer—but I decided to move along with her in this direction of her thought. We had already discussed a great deal of personal difficulty.)

I enjoy so much
the thousands of people that come up to me and say,
with tears in their eyes, thanking me for the years . . .

JC: How nice.

LB: of, of, uh, laughter and

JC: Yeah.

LB: and enjoyment that I've given them. You, you've gotta like that, gotta be crazy if you don't like that.

JC: It's amazing; it really is. This is just an aside. I've worked in hospitals, with cancer patients, and so forth. And to walk into their rooms and to see them watching your shows and to observe what it does for them is so special, it lightens their hearts and it makes the day easier.

LB: Yeah

JC: And more pleasant. . . .

(By sharing this experience with Lucy, she responded with more questions about me. This highlighted the degree of reciprocal empathy Lucy and I shared in the interview.)

LB: I think my ability can be evaluated as my making. The only luck I recognize—I don't use that word luck very often for some reason or other—
I don't
I don't know why, but if, but, if I
I have been lucky, I've been lucky in making all these crazy things I've done believable. I think it's the believability. I think my ability is believability, and people have believed, and that's why they laugh.
I tend to look at it from that that point,
uh, only,
uh, also the ability to get up and go to work, and—and to love it.

I think that is an ability in itself.

People who, who don't dig their work must, uh, be in a terrible state. And have, having a lot of energy, a great option to please people. I had that since in grade school. Always wanted to please my teachers, you know.

Does that mean anything?

(Lucy turned to me for reassurance, but I decided not to confirm her ability in an effort to see how she responded without confirmation.)

JC: Okay, did you want to say anything more about luck or your success?

LB: I don't know how to talk about luck. I've never put things down, checked them off to luck. And I don't know why.

I very seldom use the expression. I don't know why I don't.

It, isn't,

I couldn't say I don't believe in it, uh,

I guess I could say that was a lucky break. I could say that and mean it.

(She turned to me again for help. Almost imploring, she looked at me for assistance but stopped herself.)

Do you count a lot on luck? I know I shouldn't be interviewing you, but, uh

JC: Uh, no, personally I . . .

(As I began to respond, she perceived my hesitation and began answering for me.)

LB: I find other words . . .

JC: If I took, yeah, I think the word I would use in my own life would probably be *blessing*.

I don't perceive things as luck—

LB: Right.

JC: That sounds too much of a—

(Now, Lucy began completing my thoughts.)

LB: Crapshoot.

JC: Yeah, I don't like that image.

(As we laughed, we both agreed that there was more to life than "luck." After another break from our discussion, we reengaged:)

          Okay, one of the biggest changes for society has been the women's
             movement.
          What are your thoughts about the women's movement?

LB: Well, I've always been so liberated, and doing what I wanted for so long.
             That I-I-I really feel no connection to it.
          Naturally, like everyone else, I always,
          I certainly want women paid the same
          and if they are, uh, eligible
          and that's about as far as I go.
          I've been so liberated and done so many things that I wanted to do, I have no
             complaints.

JC: You never felt hampered because you were a woman.

LB: Never.

JC: Okay.

LB: I've been very happy
          I was a woman.

JC: Hm. The idea of men's roles—

LB: Often wished I was more of a woman.

JC: What do you mean by that?

LB: Oh, I don't know.
          When I was younger, I
          didn't feel as feminine and protected, I guess.

(By the expression on her face, she stunned herself by what had "slipped" out
of her mouth; she had not felt safe in her youth. On the basis of our rapport,
she felt safe enough to explore this.)

          I never have used that expression before,
          but, uh,
          I-I felt like I was on my own
          too much.
          I wished that I had
          —no one's ever said to me what you just said to me.
          No one ever asked me, uh, Did I have a helping hand right along the path.
          No one ever asked me that . . .

JC: Mm hm.

LB: and I realize that, I didn't,

male or female.

JC: So, you didn't really take on a role as the young little princess in the home.
         There wasn't this "prissy" kind of a lifestyle?

LB: Nothing,
         nothing like that.

JC: Mm hm, mm hm.

LB: None of our people are like that.
         They're all quite independent.

JC: I see.

LB: Very independent as a matter of fact.
         And, uh,
         they get the job done.

(Second excerpt)

JC: Would you be supportive of such things as the E.R.A. and the women's
         movement?

LB: I don't know that much about it.

JC: Okay.

LB: I'm, I guess I'm supportive.
         I do things for them
         wh-whoever the hell they are, and whatever the hell they're doing.

(We both laughed.)

         I don't know, but, uh,
         I remember at the beginning the burning, uh, bra times, that was disgusting
            to me.
         But I'm sure—

JC: Well, what do you think the role of a woman should be?

LB: I think first comes the home . . .

JC: Uh huh.

LB: and children
         and family.
         If you still have time to work, fine.
         And, uh,
         if it doesn't interfere with everything else, and if you need work, you should
            prepare yourself for it

and do the best you can, and get the highest wages available.
That's as far as I go with whatever you call it.

JC: Mm hm.

(We both laughed.)

LB: The women's movement.
I'm all for it because I'm one of the busiest women and have been
one of the most active,
but I just have no complaints.
I never have had.
I was awfully happy that Desi was running
things so beautifully.

JC: Okay, well, those times sound like a lot of fun since you were working at
the role of the women in the family, and then the value of what you're
saying is that the home role is a very important part of your life—

LB: Yeah . . .

JC: to be able to have the home and the family.

LB: And it's wonderful to have a record of it, too.

(Lucy referred to her volumes of home movies. Through such statements, I
felt strongly Lucy's nurturing characteristic. Her log of family history resonated with my own experience. I wanted to understand how she compared her
personal and professional achievements.)

JC: Recreated. That's excellent!
How would you define success?

LB: (Sigh) Just being happy in my work has been my success, and I've always
been happy in my work.
I never got into show business until I got out here, and I've been very happy
doing what I've been doing.
To me, that's, uh, the, I was successful long before I was "successful."

JC: Thanks. Just one last question on women's and men's roles. I was
wondering if you could respond to the changes in identity for women
and men today—
specifically, in a man—and what should he be in view of what has occurred
with the women's movement.

LB: I think it must be very difficult for the *men.*

> I feel sorry for the *young* men. The older men can take it more with a grain
> of salt and say, "Oh the hell with it." But the young men must be *very, very*
> confused. They've even lost a chase.

JC: Mm hm.

LB: And it,
> it looked good at first. It was, hmmm, "How 'bout that!"
> But it isn't turning out that way. Is it?
> You refuse to answer?

JC: I'm the interviewer—today.

(In a jovial manner, we laughed but maintained our roles. Our mutual
attunement gave us license to complete each other's thoughts, correct each
other's impressions, and speak freely.)

LB: Yes, but I—

JC: No, I certainly hear what you're saying. Sure—

LB: can tell my son and,
> uh, uh,
> his friends Dino and Billy.
> all those Steves and Stevens and boys that he runs with. Huh,
> they're all very confused,
> and they're not having as much fun as

JC: they might.

LB: I think that the—
> in my opinion . . .

(Lucy struggled to identify the essence of what she felt the women's movement may have taken away.)

LB: Isn't that something? *Romance!*
> That's a hell of a word to forget, isn't it?

JC: Beautiful word; it's a great word.

LB: I forgot it completely (laugh).
> That's awful—no, I really went blank on "romance," and I have a lot of it in
>   my life now.
> And I had none of it.
> I had bits and pieces of romance that I couldn't trust.
> We have absolute trust,

but I think that's marvelous when a man knows what he wants, and knows
how to get it, and knows how to protect—and take care of—and mostly
himself, first.

I wish my son could, uh,

could get like that. He's, he,

he could learn a lot from his stepfather. He appreciates him, but he hasn't
learned that much yet.

I had one thing in my favor: I was not too attractive, and, uh, I wasn't pounced
upon and chased around desks too much. It helped.

JC: Really.

LB: It really does.

It must be tough on girls that are very beautiful and, uh, stacked and all that.
And then they have an awful lot more to put up with. People let me get to
work (laugh).

They didn't spend their time chasing me that much.

I had a fair amount of it.

JC: I'm sure, I'm sure.

LB: But I could handle it by the time it happened.

(Lucy came through as a very traditional woman. I wanted to understand to
what degree she chose her values and to what extent she believed them
intrinsically.)

JC: Are there any other values that you would say were really

important in guiding your life and giving direction to your life or that you are
appreciative for

that you hold onto? Th-there doesn't have to be; I'm just trying to—

LB: I'm proud of the way I've brought up my children. Proud of the fact that I
make my husband happy, and several friends and acquaintances,

and that I haven't gotten into dire straits and bad trouble or made trouble for
anyone else.

I don't know what else you mean—

JC: Okay. That's good.

What gives meaning to life for you?

LB: Having people around me, comfortable, and happy. And to take care of,

I like to take care of things. I don't like to see a plant die

let alone a dog or a

human. Do I . . .

JC: Does God, does God?

LB: Do I sound trite?

JC: Oh, no. I think the important thing is to be honest about your own—

(Lucy regularly referred to the fact that she was self-conscious about her adequacy in the discussion. Although she had thoughts and feelings on these deeper matters, she had never really explored them with anyone.)

LB: I don't know any,
uh, uh,

JC: Yeah, well, whatever the answers are—

(I said this to encourage her and to engender a spontaneous response.)

LB: Maybe I sound like high school,
but I don't know any other way to do it—

JC: No, whatever is the way you think or feel.

(She regained her poise, nodding, indicating with her girlish smile that she was ready for the next issue.)

The next question I'm gonna ask is, does God have a place in your life?

LB: I think God is every living thing.
I don't think of Him as a person, although I have looked up and talked to Him.

JC: Mmm.

LB: And, yet,
when I take it apart,
I don't really think that there's a person someplace that's going to come back
to this earth and smash things, or change things, or whatever,
but there certainly are some—look, one snowflake is enough to make you
wonder.
One snowflake. There isn't another one like it.
In the world every zebra has different stripes.
There's something magic and wonderful in this nature, I guess.
This a wonderful thing!

JC: How about for you?
What's next?

LB: I'm not going to top what I've done.
That's a goal,

and, uh,
just to try to finish out my life by making those around me as comfortable
as possible, and anticipating.

JC: Uh, huh.

LB: Like, for instance, I,
I've taken people out of my will and given them now.
I don't want them waiting around for me to die.
I don't want a monetary value put on
. . . the few years I have left.

JC: Mm hm.

LB: It doesn't thrill me, the thought of it.
But I would like to give it to them now and see what they do with it,
and fine, go.
I've done it about five times.

JC: Hm.

LB: I'm doing more of it.

JC: How do you feel about that?

LB: Well, that's,
that's answering it.

JC: Okay.

LB: It's the same thing because I don't expect to get any younger or more
alive, uh,

(she laughed)

or jump any higher.
I just keep myself so that I'm not a drudge and a bore sitting around.
Too much playing backgammon.
I have to keep busy doing—

JC: Okay.

(The remainder of the interview was intensely humorous, emotional, and
searching. Several times, she shifted the attention to me.)

LB: You're some guy, John.
Y'know I'm just, I'm,
my heart's going like this.

(She moved her hand, indicating a thumping, fast rhythm of her heart to
describe the intensity she felt.)

I'm, I'm embarrassed, that I couldn't, uh,
answer, more,
uh,

JC: Well, I'm honored and thrilled to—

(She cut me off as I sought to compliment her on moving into issues this deeply.)

LB: I wish,
I-I wish I had more knowledge, of, uh, vocabulary, and what not,
but, uh,

JC: Well, the form may not be satisfactory to you, but the the power of your spirit is so clear. You are knowledgeable—

(I pressed to reassure her and observed Lucy shift from uncertainty to stability.)

LB: I hope so.

JC: It is so meaningful to so many.
I hope that you can see that.
I'm sure you see it from some letters.
I'm sure there's correspondence.
It's a wonderful thing that you've done for people.

LB: I hope so.

Elements of the I:R Approach

From my initial meeting with Lucille Ball, I felt at ease. In retrospect, we appeared to share several personal characteristics. Most prominently, we shared openness, respect, and especially nurturance. Lucy displayed her openness in the way she shared her hospitality, her home, and herself. For my part, I shared with her answers to questions about my personal life. In her treatment of me and statements about her family, Lucy nurtured her relationships.

I found Lucy to be a highly motivated, goal-oriented woman. As with her professional work, in this project, she immersed herself to attain a level of facility in which she could feel pride and accomplishment. Accordingly, she wanted to give me what I needed for this project, and she worked hard in the interviews.

In turn, I offered reassurance, acknowledgment, validation, and encouragement. With regard to respect, Lucy valued my work and expressed esteem. As Lucy disclosed intensity of her experiences, I supported her efforts while maintaining a safe, supportive structure. In fact, Lucy resonated several of the qualities I indicated in my interviewing as part of the I:R approach.

Because we established a positive rapport, we confronted difficult and problematic issues both in her personal life and in ways that challenged her position and thought. As our qualities resonated, several opportunities emerged for what I described as the "potential for action" for deepening the interview. This provided opportunities for enhancing our interaction and relationship.

In her responses to open-ended questions, we covered much material and had an enjoyable time. Whether the fact that she had a son my age (transference) or that I had watched her for many years as a maternal figure on television (countertransference) facilitated our warmth, the I:R elements identify the process of our interview. The notation of speech, following Tedlock's method of transcription, illustrates reflective and thoughtful responses rather than repetition of rehearsed script.

Self-disclosure occurred for both of us. This was not a method to deepen the relationship, but an outgrowth of the relationship. The self-disclosure exchanged illustrates the evolving relationship. Very early in the interview—in part because of her questions and prodding—I shared personal aspects of my life. When I asked her about her ethnic background, she asked about mine. When she learned I am Greek American, she recited the alphabet in Greek that she had learned as a child from her uncle and "substitute father," George Mandicos (In fact, she not only recited every letter, but also spoke with a Greek accent). Her interest in supplying me with snacks or discussing matchmaking possibilities for me confirmed our rapport and her interest in our interviews that led to intense discussions. I have already explained how Lucy pulled for protection from others. My nurturance, respect, and openness not only resonated with this need but guided her to respond in kind. After suggesting that I meet some local women (because I was not married at the time), she added protectively, "That's not such a good idea; I really don't think they're good enough for you."

At one point, she told me about her dancing ability and lifted her skirt to her hips to show me her shapely legs. And they were! The potential for action prompted by our mutual characteristics deepened the experience of these qualities. Lucy concluded our meeting by describing how involving and intense her interview had been and invited me back to continue.

In a separate project, I interviewed Desi Arnaz, Jr., Lucy's son. As he reviewed this manuscript, I pointed out that his mother's answers were very insightful. Desi said that she did not usually give answers to the personal and philosophical questions that were raised in our interviews: "Even though she was interviewed all the time, I don't remember an interview like this." He said that people really did not understand Lucy.

Desi kept saying while reading the transcripts, "That's fair—that's right!" He observed that an artist rides on a roller coaster of great highs and great lows, both manufacturing plastic and false images for the public and sometimes generating destruction for himself or herself. He said, "My mother was a mother, like yours, and she was also a very funny lady who was unbelievably believable. Because you see her as a person as well, you have the story right." Although Desi attributed authenticity to this interview, it actually resulted from the opportunity provided for Lucy to present herself through this approach.

6

Conducting the Interactive-Relational Interview

This chapter introduces how to apply the interactive-relational (I:R) approach to various settings. In particular, application is made from four separate fields: therapy, journalism, health, and business. Finally, ethical issues are examined with reference to professional boundaries and value of the person.

Applications in the Professional Settings

The I:R approach could be applied to most interviewing encounters— from personal friendships and media communication to counseling and business interactions. I:R draws from psychological aspects of interviewing—not because the I:R approach is more appropriate to clinical settings but because most journalism, business, and health books concerning interviewing primarily address techniques (how-to approaches) for data collection and do not give attention to the elements of interaction and relationship (Duncan & Fiske, 1977; Gans, 1979; Jucker, 1986; Matarazzo & Wiens, 1972). This book extends this wider perspective of interviewing the person to other interviewing fields.

The I:R approach engages a deepened communication between the interviewer and interviewee in a variety of settings. To show how a specific professional setting and this approach meet their objectives, we will consider four different arenas: therapy, journalism, health professions, and business.

THERAPY

As a patient or client enters therapy, the therapeutic dyad enables participatory exploration and consensual validation of the relationship established by therapist and patient. Although such objectives of therapy extend significantly beyond those of the I:R approach, the I:R approach provides invaluable guidelines toward establishing the tone of the relationship and building rapport through the initial interview.

In earlier chapters, we considered how formalized roles of the interviewer, directives of traditional schools in psychology (psychoanalytic, behavioral, and humanistic), and various psychological techniques and devices (empathy, listening skills, therapeutic alliance, transference, and countertransference) are distinguished from the objectives of the I:R approach. In service of therapeutic objectives, however, the I:R approach invites a genuine communication of therapist-client based on the self-awareness, authenticity, and attunement of the therapist, unbridled by formalized professionalism.

In the therapeutic setting, I:R facilitates as it identifies how an interviewer (therapist) may create effective rapport. In the discussion of the I:R approach, we have drawn upon several insights from literature in therapy to explain the significance of matching in the relationship the way that personal qualities resonate with the interviewer:interviewee, and how attunement facilitates safety and freedom for the interviewee to explore himself or herself. Such principles and dimensions establish the readiness of a therapist to engage his patient. Within the professional parameters of one's psychological approach and objectives, such a foundation sets the stage for the deeper work of therapeutic treatment.

In one example where I:R was applied in therapy, a psychologist reported on a woman in psychodynamic treatment who was trying to learn more about herself and relationships. In her interpersonal style, she gravitated to a caretaking role with most interactions, often at the cost of meeting her own needs. Predictably, she sought to take care of her therapist as well. She would ask the therapist personal questions, express interest in the clinician's well-being, and attempt to engage a caring role.

The therapist, keenly attuned to the underlying dynamic, resisted follow-up to the patient's inquiries about personal matters and guarded strictly against self-disclosure. In response, the patient viewed the clinician as non-relational and "inhospitable."

As fate had it, both the patient and the therapist were pregnant. The patient, expecting twins, was advised by her physician to stay in bed for several months before the due date. Given the backdrop of the patient's litany of complaints for not sharing personally, the clinician decided to incorporate I:R at this point, not simply revealing through self-disclosure but sharing a personal experience that was authentic and attuned to the patient's need for establishing more connection. The therapist relayed that she felt disconcerted in having to stop her usual activities for one week before her due date.

In response to this revelation, at the next session, the patient presented her therapist with a plant. When asked what prompted the patient to bring this gift, she exuberantly described that the earlier sharing made her feel genuinely connected and accepted, enhancing her ability for self-exploration. Although the patient's caretaking gesture had surfaced through the gift of the plant, the therapist and patient could now explore this personality dynamic collabora-tively and on the basis of deeper understanding.

JOURNALISM

Journalistic communication is driven by the maxim, "Get the facts." The demand toward that end is often so great that the interviewee feels trampled in this bloodthirsty quest. The interview does not need to be driven by the clock. Although the 5 Ws and H (who, what, where, when, why, and how) provide the template for a journalist's task, an aggressive, time-conscious focus may not be the only way to achieve one's end. Alternatively, attention to this template and the principles of I:R may result in a stronger interviewing experience—even under the pressure of time.

How can the journalist mediate pressuring or intruding upon an inter-viewee and maintaining a relational posture? From the I:R perspective, this clearly depends on one's personal characteristics. Journalists need not argue that they must use "offensive fact-finding" as part of the job. Through the I:R approach, they have the opportunity to draw on their own characteristics and ethics.

Shirley Biagi (1992) describes in *Interviews That Work: A Practical Guide for Journalists* a number of coercive suggestions under her recommendations for "Develop(ing) a Partnership" in telephone interviews:

> A shared goal is important in any interview . . . [quoting Bill Nottingham, an award-winning investigative reporter]. "I try to bring the person I'm talking to in as a partner on the story" (saying to the interviewee), "You can help me a lot if you'll give me accurate information," and "You don't want me to write an inaccurate story, do you? Let's work together." (p. 73)

This high-pressured maneuver has less to do with the stated collaboration than the intent to get information. The author suggests the success of such statements, but she does not address the impact of such communication on the interviewer. In the section of Biagi's book, "Prepare for 'no comment,' " she advises:

> . . . you must be especially persuasive . . . [Again, quoting Nottingham, who tells interviewees] . . . If I don't have this information in my story, it's because you didn't want to give it to me. And I'm happy to say that in my story. I'm happy to say that I called you up, Mr. Official, and you didn't want to commit. And everybody who reads the story is going to know that you could have commented if you wanted to. By saying this he usually persuades the interviewee to answer. (Biagi, 1992, p. 74)

Such reality orientation may be helpful to the interviewee and may encourage a response to tough questions. However, one may be able to offer such realistic information, for example, concerning the implications of one's inadequate responsiveness, while engaging many of the I:R aspects that may deepen the subject's response.

Biagi goes on to explain formalized and sometimes intimidating recommendations to obtain an interview, for example, "Steal some ideas from professional counselors. Face people squarely and look them in the eyes. . . . Be solicitous but not deferential" (p. 79). Likewise, John Brady (1976), in his book *The Craft of Interviewing,* proposes such maneuvers to learn about an interviewee: a "way to the interviewee's heart is through his secretary" (p. 14). Brady continues exposing the notorious manipulations of journalists and formulaic approaches. He recalls how Mike Wallace "tried to use booze to loosen the tongue of G. Gordon Liddy after arrangements had been made for an interview by CBS to discuss the Watergate break-in" (p. 61). Interestingly, Liddy didn't bite the bait—he didn't take one drink. Brady (1976) also quotes Barbara Walters's five "fool proof" questions for the overinterviewed that she shared with the *New York Times*:

1. If you were recuperating in a hospital, who would you want in the bed next to you, excluding relatives?
2. What was your first job?
3. When was the last time you cried?
4. Who was the first person you ever loved?
5. What has given you the most pleasure in the last year? (pp. 85-86)

Such contrived questioning lacks spontaneity. When asked to answer these questions, Barbara Walters said, "Uh, well . . . I don't want to. It would take too long to think of some good answers" (p. 86).

In journalism today, there exists a marked difference between entertaining and insightful interviews and sensationalized, manipulative, or contrived interviews. Tenacity and persistence have a place in all of these approaches, especially when they genuinely express one's characteristics. However, one may find it helpful to convey one's other personal characteristics and ethical stance to engage the desired interview. Importantly, the process of the interview will have a long-term impact on a journalist's reputation, success, and public perception. When people think of Diane Sawyer, Katie Couric, Bill Moyers, Sam Donaldson, or Mike Wallace, they conjure up images of an interview based on the individual styles of these specific persons or the engagements established by the particular interviewers.

Interviewing in journalism quite often involves not only gathering information or getting a story quickly but understanding people. To obtain understanding, an interviewer may well achieve his or her ends through engaging the I:R process over and against any effort that identifies the interviewee as someone whom one should manipulate, coerce, or deceive.

George Killenberg and Rob Anderson (1989) observe that a reporter needs to reflect, "What is my event?" They state, "The communication reporter will be listening at all times—to himself or herself as well as to the interviewee" (p. 10). They point out that the reluctant interviewee may be reluctant only in relationship with *this* particular interviewer; such reluctance cannot be perceived in isolation from the relationship or event in which it is experienced. In agreement with a basic premise of I:R, however, the interviewer must assume responsibility for his or her method.

HEALTH PROFESSIONS

Modern understandings of health advocate for holistic attention to the person over the Cartesian model that emphasized intellectual assessment of the patient's systems or individual parts. Physicians recognize the importance of the patient's perception of illness, taking into account the patient's ideas, feelings, fears, ability to function, and expectations. So, Rourke (1995) concludes, "Patient-centered interviewing is effective in terms of patient satisfaction and symptom resolution" (p. 69). The modern direction of thought in health care emphasizes maintenance of well-being (preventive health care) over healing pathology alone. Several epidemiological studies point to improved health outcomes when the patient participates in his or her health care and establishes positive feelings in the process of health management (e.g., hope, relational bonds with health providers, and participating in the decision-making process). Peterson and Bossio (1991) review striking examples in the literature that confirm links between psychological states and physical well-being.

The I:R approach finds a positive foil with such health care objectives. The physician who engages a solid understanding of the patient not only facilitates compliance and rapport but enhances healthful objectives.

The example of a pediatrician responding to a couple's concerns of their newborn baby's fall demonstrates vividly the application of the I:R approach for health professionals.

When an 8-month-old had fallen off the bed, a young couple feared the possibility that the baby had sustained an internal injury. Although no dramatic symptoms presented themselves and the baby was easily consoled, the couple observed that the child was unusually discomforted several hours following the accident. To be assured that there was no danger, they decided to contact a pediatrician.

Upon reporting the details to the pediatrician on call, he responded, "Well, why are you calling now, several hours after the fall?" Not waiting for a response, the doctor continued, "If the baby is not vomiting or having convulsions, what am I supposed to tell you?"

Quite put off by the physician's remarks, the husband asked the doctor if he found the call an imposition. The pediatrician responded, "No, but this doesn't sound like an emergency." The conversation ended quickly. In the end, the physician did not alleviate the parents' concern during the night.

In contrast to this pediatrician's response, an I:R exchange could have evolved, alleviating the parents immediate concerns and offering reassurance. An I:R communication may have ensued as follows:

Parent: Our child fell off the bed today and we were concerned that she may be hurt.

Physician: I'm sorry to hear that. This must have been scary for you. How is she doing at this time? And how are you managing?

Parent: She seems fine physically. She was easily soothed. There are no bruises and no distinguishing symptoms except we're finding that she has not been herself—she appears on edge—we're very concerned.

Physician: Has she vomited or convulsed?

Parent: No. Nothing like that.

Physician: I'm glad to hear that. That kind of fall would make any of us concerned. Well, it sounds like she is not in danger. These things do happen and they are understandingly disturbing. I would recommend that you continue observing her reactions, and if this edginess that you describe continues, or if other symptoms or signs appear, feel free to give me a call. If you feel that it would be helpful, of course, bring the baby into the office. Is there anything else I can do for you?

In the responses of the pediatrician, we observe not only "good bedside manners" and empathy but an attempt on the part of the physician to maintain a relationship with the parents and respond to their concerns that draws them out.

BUSINESS

Job interviews and business interviews inherently present the difficulty of balancing the power differential between the interviewer and interviewee. To address this imbalance in communication and achieve the goals of assessment, the business interviewer finds him- or herself at the helm for outcome according to his or her conduct in the interview.

Martha Komter (1991) observes that conversation with "two-way traffic" (p. 38) should result as both parties exchange information about one another. Beyond several helpful themes for both interviewer and interviewee that Komter presents (e.g., the job interview as a social encounter with its own logic, management of labor relations, and difficult communications for employees and employers), the resourcefulness of the participants as engaged in the I:R approach may greatly enhance business interactions.

Lois Einhorn, Patricia Hayes Bradley, and John E. Baird, Jr. (1982), in *Effective Employment Interviewing: Unlocking Human Potential,* take on some of the personal dilemmas of genuine communication when discussing the ethics of honesty in the interviewing setting. They point out how, in business interviews, the interviewee is asked "to expose" (p. 81) him- or herself, whereas self-disclosure of the interviewer is nonreciprocal.

In such circumstances, the interviewer may enhance communication by building the relationship through acknowledging such imbalances and the lack of reciprocity, engaging as he or she finds appropriate. By attending to the dynamics of the I:R posture, attuning to the interviewee's experience, and engaging the interviewee, the awkward distance in roles may be effectively contained. As the interviewee feels safe and attended, he or she is likely to reveal more of him- or herself—and facilitate the objective of the meeting.

Ethics

PROFESSIONAL BOUNDARIES

The I:R approach emphasizes the significance of the interviewer's involvement in the interviewing process. Topics such as interaction, relationship, self-awareness, authenticity, attunement, personal characteristics, beliefs, and values accentuate the serious degree to which one's person, as interviewer, is invested in I:R.

Some may find that this personal emphasis risks boundary violations. Certainly, drawing on a single component of I:R without an interviewer's attentiveness to attunement, sensitivity of one's impact, or an ethical sensitivity concerning people may be problematic. In fact, the most savvy and gifted interviewer may make an error in judgment. Self-awareness, attunement, and sensitivity, however, should enable the interviewer to recognize the error, apologize, and reorient him- or herself. It is hoped that both parties would benefit from the experience as he or she would grow in the interview.

The interactive and relational components are explicated here in an effort to enable the interviewer to understand an interviewee beyond merely an information-gathering context, in a manner that invites an encounter of the interviewer's feelings, values, and concerns. These objectives should not infringe on professional boundaries and personal boundaries. Nor does one need to be a senior clinician to incorporate this perspective. One may become facile with I:R as he or she would with any perspective. As documented in some of the cases of this book, I was neither a trained clinician nor a journalist when I conducted several interviews that incorporated fundamental components of I:R. Although seasoned by experiences, one cannot help but observe the effectiveness of interviewers like Bill Moyers and Katie Couric, among others, who are not trained therapists but employ personal, engaging, collaborative elements that we may find detailed in I:R.

By honestly approaching an interview without pretense of one's role, abilities, or task and genuinely engaging the I:R approach to the best of one's abilities, one could engage the foundation for a genuine encounter.

Because I:R requires the engagement of personal qualities of both interviewer and interviewee, a danger may exist for the infringement of personal and professional boundaries. Through self-awareness, ethical conduct, and clarity of professional objectives, both parties may directly address their interactions and relationship.

VALUE OF THE PERSON

Underlying the I:R approach is a fundamental affirmation of the people involved, that is, the interviewer and interviewee. I:R acknowledges the purposes for which an interview is pursued, usually to gather information. However, this approach affirms a process for ascertaining information that is genuine, forthright, and respectful.

Because this approach is based on ethical methods for obtaining information, and this holds a value of the person, critical judgment is not held in abeyance. Some may feel that because they engage a relationship or affirm principled behavior, evaluative or rigorous assessment constitutes symmetrical relationships. One may engage in a relationship and maintain critical judgment.

As previously stated, one needs to make the difficult distinction between the structure of this approach—or any theory, for that matter—and one's own subjective interpretation of and participation in that approach or theory. In this book, I have identified some of my personal qualities that characterize my adaptation of the I:R approach. Although I tried to differentiate the structure of this approach from my personal expression of the approach, I have, inevitably, influenced some of the structure. Each interviewer has the responsibility to seek clarity about the subjective and objective impact on his or her work and to acknowledge that this process, regardless of one's vigilance, nevertheless exists.

In the I:R approach for interviewing, one is encouraged to identify his or her impact in cooperation with the interviewee to participate openly in the continuously growing opportunity thereby made available by coming to understand the other human "being."

Appendix A: Assessing
Your Personal Characteristics

Listed below, you will find 100 characteristics that you may or may not feel you possess. Rate yourself on a scale of 1 to 5 for each quality. This list is not comprehensive; you can add more traits.

	High		Average		Low
	1	2	3	4	5
1. Accurate					
2. Adventuresome					
3. Alert					
4. Ambitious					
5. Analytical					
6. Amiable					
7. Articulate					
8. Artistic					

	High		Average		Low
	1	2	3	4	5
9. Assertive					
10. Athletic					
11. Attentive					
12. Attractive					
13. Brave					
14. Broad-minded					
15. Capable					
16. Cheerful					
17. Competent					
18. Competitive					
19. Confident					
20. Conscientious					
21. Consistent					
22. Constructive					
23. Cooperative					
24. Courteous					
25. Creative					
26. Decisive					
27. Dependable					
28. Detailed					
29. Determined					
30. Disciplined					
31. Efficient					
32. Empathic					
33. Emotional					
34. Energetic					
35. Enthusiastic					
36. Expressive					
37. Fair					
38. Faithful					
39. Flexible					
40. Forceful					
41. Free spirited					
42. Friendly					
43. Generous					

	High		Average		Low
	1	*2*	*3*	*4*	*5*
44. Gracious					
45. Gregarious					
46. Helpful					
47. Honest					
48. Humorous					
49. Independent					
50. Informed					
51. Innovative					
52. Insightful					
53. Inspiring					
54. Intelligent					
55. Just					
56. Kind					
57. Logical					
58. Loyal					
59. Lucid					
60. Mature					
61. Mechanical					
62. Moral					
63. Motivated					
64. Musical					
65. Nurturant					
66. Objective					
67. Optimistic					
68. Organized					
69. Outgoing					
70. Patient					
71. Perceptive					
72. Persevering					
73. Pioneering					
74. Pleasant					
75. Poised					
76. Polished					
77. Practical					
78. Principled					

	High		Average		Low
	1	2	3	4	5
79. Professional					
80. Punctual					
81. Realistic					
82. Reflective					
83. Respectful					
84. Responsible					
85. Sensitive					
86. Serious					
87. Sincere					
88. Social					
89. Spiritual					
90. Spontaneous					
91. Stable					
92. Tactful					
93. Thorough					
94. Tolerant					
95. Trusting					
96. Trustful					
97. Trustworthy					
98. Unique					
99. Versatile					
100. Other					

Appendix B:
Interviewing Data and Archives

Lucille Ball and B. F. Skinner graciously participated in extensive taped interviews with selections that I have included in this book. The conversations used in this book illustrate particular issues concerning the I:R approach. Recordings and transcripts of the interview material are dated and logged, and are available, with permission, for review. One may obtain copies of the transcripts of the interviews with Lucille Ball from:

Lucille Ball Productions, Inc.
1041 North Formosa Avenue
Los Angeles, CA 90046

and of B. F. Skinner from:

The B. F. Skinner Foundation, Inc.
P.O. Box 825
Cambridge, MA 02238

The comprehensive collection of data, tapes, and verbatims of these interviews, in addition to the tape recordings and transcripts of the participants for
the study *Women, Motivation and Success,* may be obtained with permission,
from the author.

The transcripts used in this study include:

1. Lucille Ball: Initial Interview, April 15, 1982
2. B. F. Skinner: November, 1972
   January, 1977
   February, 1977
   December 29, 1986
   December 18, 1987

Plans are also underway to house copies of these interviews at

The Henry Murray Research Center
Radcliffe College
Cambridge, MA 02138

Appendix C:
Bibliography

Allport, G. (1968). *The person in personality.* Boston: Beacon Press.

Barrand, A. G. (1988). The kizaemon tea bowl: A perceptual gauntlet which has not been picked up. *The Studio Potter, 17,* 27-31.

Biagi, S. (1992). *Interviews that work: A practical guide for journalists.* Belmont, CA: Wadsworth.

Bowen, M. (1978). *Family therapy in clinical practice.* New York: Jason Aronson.

Bowlby, J. (1969). *Attachment and loss: Vol. 1. Attachment.* New York: Basic Books.

Brady, J. (1976). *The craft of interviewing.* Cincinnati, OH: Writer's Digest.

Brey, C. D. (1985). *Analyzing the psychotherapist's interpretation of counsellor nonverbal behavior.* Doctor of Psychology research paper, Biola University.

Brusselman, C. (1980). *Toward moral and religious maturity.* Glenview, IL: Silver Burdett.

Carini, P. F. (1979). *The art of seeing and the visibility of the person.* Grand Forks: University of North Dakota, North Dakota Study Group on Evaluation.

Casement, P. J. (1991). *Learning from the patient.* New York: Guilford.

Chirban, J. T. (1981). *Human growth and faith: Intrinsic and extrinsic motivation in human development.* Washington, DC: University Press of America.

Chirban, J. T. (1990). *The interactive-relational approach to interviewing: Application with Lucille Ball and B. F. Skinner.* Ann Arbor, MI: University Microfilms International.

Chirban, S. S. (1993). *Correlates of oneness motivation in adulthood: A longitudinal perspective.* Ann Arbor, MI: University Microfilms International.

Colson, D. B., Horowitz, L., Allen, J. G., Frieswy, K., Siebalt, H., et al. (1988). Patient collaboration as a criterion for the therapeutic alliance. *Psychoanalytic Psychology, 5,* 259-268.

Cooper, J. O., Heron, T. E., & Heword, W. L. (1987). *Applied behavior analysis.* Columbus, OH: Merrill.

DeAngelis, T. (1989, December). Countertransference disclosure is debated. *American Psychoanalytical Association Monitor,* p. 24.

Derlega, V. J., & Berg, J. H. (1987). *Self-disclosure: Theory, research, and therapy.* New York: Plenum.

Derlega, V. J., Matts, S., Petronio, S., & Margulis, S. (1993). *Self-disclosure.* Newbury Park, CA: Sage.

DeVoge, J. T., & Beck, S. (1978). The therapist-client relationship in behavior therapy. In M. Hernson, R. M. Eisler, & P. M. Miller (Eds.), *Progress in behavior modification* (pp. 203-248). New York: Academic Press.

Duncan, S., & Fiske, D. W. (1977). *Face to face interaction: Research and theory.* Hillsdale, NJ: Lawrence Erlbaum.

Eichenbaum, L., & Orbach, S. (1982). *Understanding women: A feminist psychoanalytic approach.* New York: Basic Books.

Einhorn, L. J., Bradley, P. H., & Baird, J. E., Jr. (1982). *Effective employment interviewing: Unlocking human potential.* Glenview, IL: Scott, Foresman.

Emmanuel, E. J., & Dubler, N. N. (1995, January 25). Presenting the physician-patient relationship in the era of managed care. *Journal of the American Medical Association,* pp. 273, 323-329.

Erikson, E. (1964). *Childhood and society.* New York: W. W. Norton.

Feiner, K., & Kiersky, S. (1994). Empathy: A common ground. *Psychoanalytic Dialogues, 4,* 425-440.

Ford, J. D. (1978). Therapeutic relationship in behavior therapy: An empirical analysis. *Journal of Consulting and Clinical Psychology, 46,* 1302-1314.

Friend, M., & Cook, L. (1992). *Interactions: Collaboration skills for school professionals.* New York: Longman.

Gans, H. J. (1979). *Deciding what's news: A study of "CBS Evening News," "NBC Nightly News," "Newsweek," and "Time."* New York: Pantheon.

Giannandrea, V., & Murphy, K. C. (1973). Similarity self-disclosure and return for a second interview. *Journal of Counseling Psychology, 10,* 545-548.

Gill, M. M. (1989). *Analysis of transference: Volume 1—Theory and technique.* Madison, CT: International University Press.

Gilligan, C. (1982). *In a different voice.* Cambridge, MA: Harvard University Press.

Giovacchini, P. L. (1972). Interpretation and definition of the analytic setting. In P. L. Giovacchini (Ed.), *Tactics and techniques in the psychoanalytic setting.* New York: Science House.

Gladstein, G. A., Brennan, J., Feldstein, J., Gladstein, G. A., Ham, M., Kreiser, J., & MacKrell, S. (1987). Empathy and counseling: Exploration in theory and research. London: Springer-Verlag.

Goldstein, E. G. (1994). Self-disclosure in treatment: What therapists do and don't talk about. *Clinical Social Work Journal, 22.*

Harvard Mental Health Newsletter. November, 1989.

Hoffman, M. A., & Spencer, G. P. (1977). Effect of interviewer self-disclosure and interviewer-subject sex pairing on perceived and actual subject behavior. *Journal of Counseling Psychology, 24,* 389-390.

Hoffman-Graff, M. A. (1977). Interviewers' use of positive and negative self-disclosure and interviewer-subject pairing. *Journal of Counseling Psychology, 24,* 184-190.

Holdstock, T. L., & Rogers, C. R. (1977). Person-centered theory. In R. J. Corini (Ed.), *Current personality theories* (pp. 125-151). Itasca, IL: Peacock.

Holstein, J. A., & Gubrium, J. F. (1995). *The active interview.* Thousand Oaks, CA: Sage.

Hutchins, D. E. (1984). Improving the counseling relationship. *Personnel and Guidance Journal, 62,* 572-575.

Ivey, A. E., Ivey, M. B., & Browning, L. S. (1993). *Counseling and psychotherapy: A multicultural perspective.* Boston: Allyn & Bacon.

Jordan, J. (1991). The relational self: A new perspective for understanding women's development. In J. Strauss & G. Goethals (Eds.), *The self: Interdisciplinary approaches.* Cambridge, MA: Harvard University Press.

Jucker, A. H. (1986). *News interviews: A pragmalinguistic analysis.* Philadelphia: John Benjamins.

Kantrowitz, J. (1986). The role of the patient-analyst "match" in the outcome of psychoanalysis. *Annals of Psychoanalysis, 14,* 273-297.

Katz, R. L. (1963). *Empathy, its nature and uses.* Glencoe, IL: Free Press.

Kiesler, D. J. (1988). *Therapeutic metacommunication.* San Antonio, TX: Consulting Psychologists Press.

Killenberg, G. M., & Anderson, R. (1989). *Before the story: Interviewing and communications skills for journalists.* New York: St. Martin's.

Kilpatrick, W. (1975). *Identity and intimacy.* New York: Delta.

Klein, J. G., & Friedlander, M. A. (1987). Test of two competing explanations for the attraction-enhancing effects of counselor self-disclosure. *Journal of Counseling and Development, 66,* 82-85.

Kohut, H. (1977). *The restoration of the self.* New York: International Universities Press.

Kohut, H. (1982). Introspection, empathy, and the semi-circle of mental health. *International Journal of Psychoanalysis, 63,* 395-407.

Komter, M. (1991). *Conflict and cooperation in job interviews: A study of talk, tasks and ideas.* Philadelphia: John Benjamins.

Lambert, M. J. (1989). The individual therapist's contribution to psychotherapy process and outcome. *Clinical Psychology Review, 9,* 469-485.

Langs, R. (1978). *The listening process.* New York: Jason Aronson.

Luborsky, L., Critts-Cristoph, P., McLellan, T., Woody, G., Piper, W., Liberman, B., Imber, S., & Pilkonis, P. (1986). Do therapists vary much in findings from four outcome studies? *American Journal of Orthopsychiatry, 56,* 501-512.

Mallinckrodt, B., & Helms, J. H. (1986). Effect of disabled counselors' self-disclosures on client perspections of the counselor. *Journal of Counseling Psychology, 38,* 343-348.

Mann, B., & Murphy, K. C. (1975). Timing of self-disclosure, reciprocity, of self-disclosure, and reactions to an initial interview. *Journal of Counseling Psychology, 22,* 204-308.

Matarazzo, J. D., & Wiens, A. N. (1972). *The interview: Research on its anatomy and structure.* Chicago: Aldine-Atherton.

Matthews, B. (1988). The role of the therapist self-disclosure in psychotherapy: A survey of therapists. *American Journal of Psychotherapy, 42,* 521-531.

McCounaughly, E. A. (1987). The person of the therapists in psychotherapeutic practice. *Psychotherapy, 24,* 303-314.

McCracken, G. (1988). *The long interview.* Newbury Park, CA: Sage.

McV. Hunt, T. (1965). Intrinsic motivation and its role in psychological development. *Nebraska Symposia on Motivation,* pp. 189-282.

Mearns, D., & Thorne, B. (1988). The "health revolution" between counselor and client. In *Person-centered counseling in action* (pp. 28-34). London: Sage.

Messer, S. B. (1986, November). Behavioral and psychoanalytic perspectives at therapeutic choice points. *American Psychologist,* pp. 1261-1272.

Miller, J. B. (1976). *Toward a new psychology of women.* Boston: Beacon Press.

Mitchell, S. (1988). *Relational concepts in psychoanalysis: An integration.* Cambridge, MA: Harvard University Press.

Minuchin, S., & Fishman, H. C. (1981). *Family therapy techniques.* Cambridge, MA: Harvard University Press.

Mollon, P. (1986). Narcissistic vulnerability and the fragile self: A failure in mirroring. *British Journal of Medical Psychology, 59,* 317-324.

Morrison, J. (1995). *The first interview.* New York: Guilford.

Murphy, K. C., & Scasz, S. R. (1972). Some effects of similarity self-disclosure. *Journal of Counseling Psychology, 19,* 121-124.

Nilsson, D., Strassberg, D. S., & Bannon, J. (1979). Perceptions of counselor self-disclosure: An analogue study. *Journal of Counseling Psychology, 19,* 121-124.

Oakley, A. (1981). Interviewing women: A contradiction in terms. In H. Roberts (Ed.), *Doing feminist research* (pp. 30-61). London: Routledge & Kegan Paul.

Olds, J., & Olds, M. (1965). *Drives, rewards and the brain.* New York: Holt, Rinehart & Winston.

Paolino, T. (1982). The therapeutic relationship in psychoanalysis. *Contemporary Psychoanalysis, 18,* 218-234.

Patterson, C. H. (1984, Winter). Empathy, warmth and genuineness in psychotherapy: A review of reviews. *Psychotherapy, 4,* 431-438.

Peca-Baker, T. A., & Friedlander, M. L. (1989). Why are self-disclosing counselors attractive? *Journal of Counseling and Development, 67,* 279-282.

Personal Narratives Group. (1989). *Interpreting women's lives.* Bloomington: Indiana University Press.

Peterson, C., & Bossio, L. M. (1991). *Health and optimism.* New York: Free Press.

Racker, H. (1987). *Transference and countertransference.* Madison, CT: International Universities Press.

Reinharz, S. (1992). *Feminist methods of social research.* New York: Oxford University Press.

Rogers, C. R. (1951). *Client-centered therapy: Its current practice, implications, and theory.* Boston: Houghton Mifflin.

Rogers, C. R. (1980). *A way of being.* Boston: Houghton Mifflin.

Rourke, J. T. D. (1995). The art and process of patient-centered interviewing. *Humane Medicine, 11,* 66-69.

Safran, J. D., McMain, S., Crocker, P., & Murray, P. (1990). Therapeutic alliance rupture as a therapy event for empirical investigation. *Psychotherapy, 27.*

Satir, V., Stachowick, J., & Taschman, H. A. (1980). *Helping families to change.* New York: Jason Aronson.

Schwartz, W. (1984). The two concepts of action and responsibility in psychoanalysis. *Journal of the American Psychoanalytic Association, 32,* 557-572.

Skinner, B. F. (1953). *Science and human behavior.* New York: Free Press.

Skinner, B. F. (1971). *Beyond freedom and dignity.* New York: Knopf.

Skinner, B. F. *Personal Correspondence.* June 30, 1989.

Skinner, B. F. (1989). The place of feeling in the analysis of behavior. In *Recent issues in the analysis of behavior.* Columbus, OH: Merrill.

Stern, D. (1985). *The interpersonal world of the infant: A view from psychoanalysis and developmental psychology.* New York: Basic Books.

Stolorow, R. D., & Brandchaft, B. (1987). Developmental failure and psychic conflict. *Psychoanalytic Psychology, 4,* 241-253.

Stolorow, R. D. (1991). Chapter 2 in R. Curtis (Ed.), *The relational self: Theoretical convergences in psychoanalysis and social psychology.* New York: Guilford.

Strupp, H. (1986). The nonspecific hypothesis of therapeutic effectiveness: A current assessment. *American Journal of Orthopsychiatry, 56,* 513-520.

Tansey, M. (1989). *Understanding countertransference: From projective identification to empathy.* Hillsdale, NJ: Analytic Press.

Tedlock, D. (1985). Reading the *Popul Vuh* over the shoulder of a diviner finding out what's so funny. *Popul Vuh: The Mayan book of dawn of life.* New York: Simon and Schuster.

Tedlock, D. (1988). *The spoken word and the work of interpretation.* Philadelphia: University of Pennsylvania Press.

Teyber, E. (1988). *Interpersonal process in psychotherapy.* Chicago: Dorsey.

Underwood, R. L. (1984). *Empathy and confrontation in pastoral care.* Philadelphia: Fortress.

VandeCreek, L., & Angstadt, L. (1985). Client preferences and applications about self-disclosure. *Journal of Counseling Psychology, 32,* 206-214.

Weinberg, G. (1984). *The heart of psychotherapy.* New York: St. Martin's.

Winnicott, D. W. (1971). *Playing and reality.* New York: Routledge.

Wolf, E. S. (1983). Concluding statement. In A. Goldberg (Ed.), *The future of psychoanalysis: Essays in honor of Heinz Kohut.* New York: International Universities Press.

Zima, J. P. (1983). *Interviewing: Key to effective management.* Washington, DC: Science Research Associates.

Index

Observational self, 8, 9
O'Connor, Sandra, 43, 44, 45, 46
Olds, J., 69
Openness, 4, 6, 7, 27, 30, 48, 81, 87, 90, 98, 115
Orientation to the present, 14, 15

Paolino, Thomas, 31
Patterson, C. H., 27
Peca-Baker, Theresa, 33, 34, 39
Perception, 17, 20, 22, 39, 53, 97, 123, 124
Person orientation, 10
Personal characteristics, 4, 6, 19, 41, 43, 47, 48, 53, 87, 115
Personal Narratives Group, 26
Peterson, Christopher, 124
Posturing, 8, 57, 84
Potential for action, 11, 12, 13, 14, 15, 16, 42, 43, 47, 48, 57
Professionalism, 4
Psychoanalysis, 17, 19, 31
Psychoanalytic theory, 20, 34

Racker, H., 31
Rapport, 38, 57, 68, 88, 89, 90, 93, 108, 111, 116, 120, 124
Reciprocation, 10, 57
Reciprocity, 34, 42
Reinharz, S., 25
Relational psychology, 17, 20, 34
Resonate, 6, 12, 87, 103
Rogerian theory, 19
Rogers, Carl, 19, 27, 28, 30, 40
Rourke, James, 124

Safran, Jeremy, 29
Satir, Virginia, 29, 32

Schwartz, W., 20
Self-awareness, 3, 4, 5, 7, 11, 14, 39, 42, 43, 51, 53, 127
Self-disclosure, 5, 11, 32, 33, 34, 39, 78, 116, 121, 126
Self-knowledge, 4, 39
Setting, 6, 10, 12, 39, 40, 45, 54, 55, 87
Shared space, 7
Skinner, B. F., 21, 24, 50, 52, 57, 64, 65, 83
Stern, Daniel, 42
Stolorow, Robert, 42
Strupp, Hans, 35
Summer, Donna, 48, 52

Tansey, Michael, 33
Tedlock, Dennis, 24
Teyber, Edward, 36
Theoretical model, 63
Therapeutic alliance, 29, 30, 31
Therapy, 2, 31, 32, 34, 35, 55, 65, 119, 120
Transference, 8, 9, 21, 30, 31, 116, 120
Translation, 17, 20, 24, 83, 89

Unconditional, positive regard, 19

Values, 4, 54, 112
VandeCreek, Leon, 33, 34, 39

Weinberg, George, 29, 31
Winnicott, Donald, 10
Wolf, E. S., 20
Women's studies, 17, 20, 25

Zima, Joseph, 27

About the Author

John T. Chirban, Ph.D., Th.D., serves as a psychologist at Harvard Medical School in the Behavioral Medicine Program at The Cambridge Hospital. As a lecturer and teacher, Dr. Chirban addresses interdisciplinary subjects in medicine, psychology, and religion. As an author and scholar, he has published academic works in ethics, psychotherapy, and psychohistory. He is director of Cambridge Counseling Associates, and he also serves as chairman of the Department of Human Development and professor of psychology at Hellenic College and Holy Cross School of Theology. Dr. Chirban holds a doctorate in clinical psychology and oral histories from Boston University's University Professors Program and a doctorate in applied theology from Harvard University.

144